ISO9000
BS5750
MADE EASY

ISO9000 BS5750

MADE EASY

A PRACTICAL GUIDE TO QUALITY

KIT SADGROVE

KOGAN
PAGE

To Alexandra, a woman of quality.

First published in 1994

Kogan Page Limited
120 Pentonville Road
London N1 9JN

©Kit Sadgrove, 1994

British Library Cataloguing in Publication Data

A CIP record for this book is available from the British Library.

ISBN 0 7494 1275 5

Typeset by Books Unlimited (Nottm), Sutton-in-Ashfield NG17 1AL
Printed in England by Clays Ltd, St Ives plc

CONTENTS

◆

Acknowledgements   8

Shedding light on the subject   9

1   **Working for a company without systems**   11

2   **What is ISO 9000?**   14

Quality: an over-used word   14
Why prevention is better than cure   14
So what exactly is ISO 9000?   17
The main points of ISO 9000   18
The problems that companies face with ISO 9000   19
The constituent parts   22
Other parts of ISO 9000   22
How standards won the Battle of Waterloo   23
Summary   24

3   **Separating fact from fiction**   25

Five complaints about ISO 9000   25
Six myths about ISO 9000   28
The real advantages and disadvantages of ISO 9000   30
The disadvantages of ISO 9000   35
Summary   38

4   **Going for ISO 9000**   39

The organisations you will meet   39
Implementing the system   41
Creating a plan   48
Starting a benchmark   48
Summary   49

5   **The right approach**   51

Certifying the right part of your business   51

Which departments to choose   52
Which part of the Standard should you apply for?   53
Advantages of doing it yourself   57
Ready-made manuals   57
Using a consultancy   58
Consultancy problems   59
How to assess a consultancy   59
Action List: checking a consultancy   60
Summary   61

6   The secrets of ISO 9000   62

Cracking the code   62
The seven principles of ISO 9000   62
Setting up a manual   64
Writing procedures   70
Summary   71

7   Improve your purchasing and design   72

The hidden structure of ISO 9000   72
Improving the quality of your suppliers   74
Looking after other people's goods   77
Getting your designs right first time   78
Summary   80

8   Managing your work   81

Checking the order   81
Managing the work   83
Reducing errors through better inspection   85
Handling and storing your product   90
Enhanced servicing   91
Summary   91

9   Helping your staff perform better   92

Defining people's roles   92
Choosing a quality manager   94
The work of the quality manager   94
Involving top management in managing the system   95
Training and communication   96
Summary   100

10   Controlling your system   **101**

The benefits of controlling important documents   101
Only include what you must   103
Learning from your mistakes   106
Summary   109

11   How to audit   **110**

The three main types of audit   110
Selecting internal auditors   111
How to set up an audit plan   112
How to carry out an audit   113
Summary   118

12   Better information   **119**

Identifying your product   119
Keeping a record   121
Learning by numbers   123
Measure your cost of quality   124
Summary   125

13   Getting registered   **126**

How to choose a certification body   126
What happens during the assessment   128
Why do they do it?   133
The benefits to your business   134
The reasons why companies fail   134
Summary   135

14   Building on your system   **136**

Surveillance visits   136
How to promote your success   136
Building on ISO 9000   138
Summary   140

Appendix 1   Translation   *143*
Appendix 2   Jargon beater   *157*
Appendix 3   Where to get help   *162*
Appendix 4   Checklist   *176*

Index   *183*

ACKNOWLEDGEMENTS

◆

A number of people gave me their time and their views on ISO 9000 (BS 5750). I would like to thank Val Harris of J. Murphy & Sons, Chris Cleasby of Fridays, Peter Gavin of Siemens Lighting, and Geoff Tyler of Concentric Pressed Products.

My grateful thanks are also due to John Taylor of Norgren Martonair, Ralph Hepworth and Jim Brownless of P-E International, Robbie Lloyd of Outset, and Barry Holland of SGS Yarsley. Any errors are my responsibility alone.

I would also like to thank my wife and children, and my parents, Victor and Rhona, for their continued support.

For the sake of simplicity, the pronoun 'he' has been used throughout this book as shorthand for 'he or she'.

If you would like help in introducing ISO 9000 (BS 5750), you can contact me at Honeycombe House, Bagley, Wedmore BS28 4TD.

Kit Sadgrove

SHEDDING LIGHT ON THE SUBJECT

◆

Are you unsure about ISO 9000? Have you heard conflicting reports about its value? Perhaps you've even heard stories about ruinous cost, bureaucracy and paper mountains?

Or maybe you're working for an organisation that has a quality assurance system, and you need to understand what it means.

If you are in that position, this is the book for you.

ISO 9000/BS 5750 Made Easy concentrates on the questions that people have when they first get involved with ISO 9000.

What this book will tell you

This book covers three important areas:

1. *What are the real benefits (and problems) of ISO 9000?* Many companies seek registration to satisfy a big customer. That is a valid reason for getting ISO 9000. But there are *other* benefits that ISO 9000 brings, some of which only become apparent after the system has been introduced.

2. *What do the words of the standard mean?* The language of the standard can seem obscure. Yet many of the complex issues in ISO 9000 are quite simple. For example, take the following clause:

   The responsibility, authority and the interrelation of all people who manage, perform and verify work affecting quality shall be defined.

   This is a formal way of saying: 'You must have an organisation chart'.

3. *How do you become registered?* In the world of ISO 9000, you will meet certification bodies, management consultancies and various other organisations. This book aims to explain what you can expect, and how to maximise your chances of getting a certificate. It also seeks to dispel some myths.

   For example, you have a choice of certification bodies with whom to register. Some are better than others for your particular business, and you can shop around to get the best value for money.

How the book will benefit you

Armed with the knowledge from this book, you will know whether ISO 9000 is right for your business. You will be able to participate in quality meetings. And you won't feel intimidated by those with apparently expert knowledge. You'll also be able to design a better system.

For some companies, ISO 9000 produces real advantages. It can save money. It can forestall errors. It can even reduce stress among staff because they know what is expected of them. *ISO 9000/ BS 5750 Made Easy* will explain how the Standard produces these advantages.

But for the unwary there are pitfalls. You can select the wrong consultant. You can design a bureaucratic system. And you can introduce a system that your workforce hates.

By reading this book you can avoid these problems. *ISO 9000/ BS 5750 Made Easy* could save your organisation thousands of pounds, and a lot of headaches.

The management tool that beats the rest

New management fads are always being launched. There is business process re-engineering, category management, and partnership sourcing. Yet ISO 9000 encompasses all these ideas. You can use it to improve communication, to get better design, and get closer to your customers.

ISO 9000 is such a widely-used tool, and one that is often so poorly implemented, that its many virtues are easily overlooked. It has brought many companies back from the brink, as the case histories in this book show. Taken seriously, it could help your organisation become more successful than you ever thought possible.

1

WORKING FOR A COMPANY WITHOUT SYSTEMS

◆

You set off for work on Monday morning. It's a fine day, and this week you're determined to create change. But fate has other things in mind for you.

As soon as you reach your desk, the problems start to arrive.

- Sales are down again. Some of your colleagues blame the state of the market. You aren't so sure; you suspect you're losing out to competitors.
- A major new product launch is on hold. A manager left last week, and the department can't work out what stage the project had reached.
- You receive a questionnaire from your biggest customer. They want to know if you have ISO 9000. They prefer to buy from registered suppliers. This could be the end of your relationship with them.
- Two hours' production lie awaiting a decision. Someone assembled the product wrongly, and the whole morning's work will have to be re-checked.
- Glancing through the window, you see a lorry unloading what seem to be crates of your product returned from a major customer.
- You work for an hour on a project. Later, a passing colleague points out that Engineering had produced a revised version a week ago. Hadn't you heard that the project was now substantially different? You groan at the thought of all that time you've wasted.
- A customer rings up looking for information on his order. No one seems to know anything about it. There is a small panic.
- The samples you ordered arrive. Opening the packaging, you find the wrong goods have been delivered. 'Surely we got the details right in the purchase order?' you ask yourself.
- The Sales Manager passes your office, looking gloomy. 'We've just lost another customer to the Japanese,' he says. 'Customers today are fed up with rubbish that Production pushes out the door. They don't have to accept those standards any more.'
- This is no way to run a railroad, you tell yourself. There must be a better way of managing the business. You seem to go from one crisis to another. There are always panics.

Does any of this seem familiar to you? Lots of little problems and a few big ones? Time wasted while mistakes are rectified? Nothing seems to go right.

All these problems have a common root – a lack of systems. Faced with this situation, some organisations turn to ISO 9000 (BS 5750). It is a system that could bring a sense of order to your business, and prevent these problems from happening.

But the problems don't just apply to manufacturing companies. Service organisations have the same symptoms, and sometimes more of them.

- Customers are disappointed because your service isn't as good as they hoped.
- You cancel an invoice because a client complains.
- Different branches do the same work in different ways, so you lose any claim to offer a consistent service.
- Work goes out in a haphazard way without being checked.
- No one seems to be responsible for co-ordination, so projects fall behind.
- Staff have to re-do work because it wasn't done properly first time.
- Different departments refuse to talk to each other.
- You endlessly tell junior staff the answer to the same old questions. As soon as one person leaves, you have to start all over again.

Note that we have hardly mentioned the word 'quality'. On first glance, many of the problems are not related to quality. But all of them affect the quality of your product or service.

ISO 9000 (BS 5750) could help your business run more smoothly. It could make you better organised and more consistent.

This book looks at how ISO 9000 works. In particular, it tries to explain how it might work for you. It also asks you for your input, starting right now.

How do quality failures manifest themselves in your organisation? Is it customer complaints, work done late, promises not kept, or customers

Table 1.1 The main problem areas in our business

Examples of quality failures in our organisation	What causes these failures?

getting less than they expected? Write down your thoughts in the box below. Then say what causes these failures.

By the time you finish *ISO 9000/ BS 5750 Made Easy*, you should have built up a picture of your quality problems, and the ways you can overcome them.

2

WHAT IS ISO 9000?

◆

In this chapter, you'll discover:

- What ISO 9000 (BS 5750) means by the word 'quality'.
- Why prevention is better than cure.
- What exactly ISO 9000 is, and how it works.
- The problems that companies face with the Standard.
- A potted history of ISO 9000.
- The constituent parts of the Standard.

QUALITY: AN OVER-USED WORD

There are 2,231 words to mean drunk, according to American wordsmith Paul Dickson. But there is only one main word for quality. That means it's an over-used term.

When ISO 9000 (BS 5750) talks about quality, it means that *your product should be fit for its intended purpose*. Quality means meeting customers' needs.

For ISO 9000, quality doesn't mean 'excellence'. This is quite a shock for people used to reading advertisements where manufacturers boast about the quality of their disc drives or their meat pies.

A Mini Metro and a Rolls Royce have different levels of refinement. One is much cheaper than the other. But both serve perfectly the needs of their customers. The owners simply have different needs. For ISO 9000, both are quality products (as long as they don't break down).

WHY PREVENTION IS BETTER THAN CURE

There are three ways you can manage quality. They are prevention, inspection and failure (see Table 2.1).

Few manufacturers carry out *no checks on quality*. But defective products regularly reach the customer. Perhaps the inspector left work early. Perhaps he omitted to check a batch. Or perhaps he checked one in three boxes, and the defects were in the other two boxes.

Many service companies carry out no quality checks. They assume that their staff will carry out the work properly. After all, many of their staff are highly trained or have professional qualifications.

Table 2.1 Quality assurance emphasises planning

THE THREE MAIN TYPES OF QUALITY MANAGEMENT					
Strategy	**Method**	**Cost**	**Timing of quality checks**	**Management style**	**Planning**
Prevention	Quality assurance (ISO 9000)	Cheap ▲	Early ▲	Proactive ▲	Planned ▲
Inspection	Quality control				
Failure	No checks on quality	▼ Expensive	▼ Late	▼ Reactive	▼ Unplanned

The problems that inspectors can't solve

Inspection is the strategy once favoured by manufacturers, and involves appointing quality inspectors. Their job is to check for defective products *after* they have been made. Typically they inspect a sample of the product, opening one box in a hundred, or standing at the end of a line watching for the broken biscuits. It doesn't stop defective products being made, so it doesn't tackle the real problems. It merely treats their symptoms.

With an inspection system, the workforce feels less need to check their own work. That is the inspectors' job. Apart from the inspectors, no one worries about what is being made.

Inspection is surprisingly poor at picking out failures. Research shows that even the best inspectors can't identify every defective item. And once a component is fitted inside another, you may no longer be able to inspect it. There is an old and inelegant saying, 'Quality can't be inspected into a product, it must be manufactured into it'. Hence the need for quality assurance (QA).

Quality assurance emphasises the need to plan quality into the work you do. It promotes the need to forestall faults. It operates in a systematic way. ISO 9000 (BS 5750) is the internationally agreed method for implementing a quality assurance system.

ISO 9000 stems from the work of people who identified the most usual causes of quality problems, and created a system to overcome them. Table 2.2 shows common quality faults, and indicates how ISO 9000 prevents them happening.

Table 2.2 How quality problems are resolved by a quality assurance system

SOLVING QUALITY PROBLEMS	
Typical quality problem	**How ISO 9000 (BS 5750) solves the problem**
Staff make mistakes because they haven't been properly trained	You ensure that everyone knows what their job is, and how to do it
Different people make the same product in their own way, causing variations in product quality	You adopt best practice in doing a job, and consistently use it
People produce the wrong goods because they are using an out-of-date specification	You ensure that everyone uses the current version of a document
Mistakes are made because the right person wasn't involved in a decision	You specify who will be responsible for quality
Different departments don't talk to each other (for example marketing and design)	You ensure communication and co-operation between staff
People don't see quality as their responsibility	You place responsibility for quality on those who produce the product
Faulty products are delivered to the customer	You carry out proper inspection checks
When found, mistakes go uncorrected, and the same mistakes are regularly made	You analyse product faults, correct them, and try to prevent them happening again

You might notice that the *quality assurance* system shown above includes some *quality control* – the carrying out of regular inspection. ISO 9000 takes quality control and adds an element of planning.

Some people refer to QA and QC as the same thing. Terminology is one of the many problems that affect this area.

Case history: From black hole to nice workplace

Norgren Martonair introduced ISO 9000 in its Kenilworth, Warwickshire plant three years ago. A £55 million company, Norgren Martonair makes a range of valves for industry, especially car manufacturers. A metal cutting business, it uses steel, brass, aluminium and cast iron.

John Taylor, its Quality Development Manager, says: 'At first there was a lot of resistance. But you have to win them over: you can't do ISO 9000 on your own. I used to have 15 inspectors, but now I have 150 – the whole workforce. And there are benefits they can see. It used to be like a black hole working in here. We've invested the savings so that it's a nice place to work.

'Now, the company has a system we're in control of. Before, the system had control of us. ISO 9000 highlights where we're doing things twice. It eliminates re-work. Corrective actions are the real benefits – it's the elimination of error.'

Management guru Tom Peters echoes John Taylor's point. 'A management system is a must', he says. 'In order to have quality throughout the organisation, you must have a guiding system that is followed passionately. Most quality programs fail because they lack either a system or passion, or both.'

SO WHAT EXACTLY IS ISO 9000?

There are three elements to ISO 9000.

1. *You say what you're going to do*. This means stating in writing how work is processed through your business. With ISO 9000, assembling a motor or producing a report is done in a standard, consistent way. You should look on it as turning best practice into normal practice.
2. *You do it*. Having defined in writing how work *should* be processed, you make sure this actually happens. You make sure that jobs are done the right way. This means using the same procedures.
   It also means that everyone is trained, and that everyone works from the current issue of the work instructions.
3. *You prove that you've done it*. This means keeping proper records. And it means doing audits to check what has been done.

Case history: The cellular telephone company that had its wires crossed.

A leading cellular telephone company decided to systemise its business by introducing ISO 9000.

Despite its high-tech and efficient image, the company had a complete lack of systems, and the work was chaotic and haphazard. Communication was particularly poor. As a result, work was often re-done several times. Customer complaints were high.

It implemented ISO 9000, and then decided to move its business two hundred miles north. Most of the staff decided not to move – which you might think would have been disastrous.

In fact, the company found it only needed 120 staff compared with the 200 it had previously employed. 40 per cent of the staff were needed solely to solve problems caused by the lack of systems.

THE MAIN POINTS OF ISO 9000

Here are the main points of ISO 9000. Most of the points are explained in more detail later in the book.

■ The Standard is called BS 5750 in the UK, EN 29000 in the EC, and ISO 9000 worldwide. They are simply different titles for the same standard.

■ ISO 9000 is a formal management system, which you adapt to meet your company's needs.

■ It is an internationally-accepted standard.

■ ISO 9000 is simply common sense set down on paper in an organised way.

■ It has been broken down into twenty headings to enable companies to implement it easily and efficiently.

■ ISO 9000 is flexible, and has been implemented by manufacturers, local government, hospitals and accountancy practices.

■ With ISO 9000, you put your existing procedures and practices down on paper. During this process, you may find that there are gaps in people's understanding of how some tasks should be undertaken. This process – of uncovering uncertainties and removing them – is usually very helpful.

- ISO 9000 makes sure that your organisation produces its work in a systematic and planned way. It encourages checking and good communication.
- Once you have installed the system, you can ask an independent organisation (called a certification body) to do an audit. If you satisfy this auditor, you receive a certificate. It proves you have a system that conforms to ISO 9000.
- The certificate demonstrates to your customers that you are committed to quality, and that you can meet their standards.
- Some companies buy only from suppliers registered to ISO 9000.

THE PROBLEMS THAT COMPANIES FACE WITH ISO 9000

ISO 9000 is not easy to understand. Many managers are expected to know what it means, but they haven't had it explained to them. That means there is a lot of confusion about it.

Even where ISO 9000 has been installed in a business, there is no obvious sign of its existence, apart from the certificate in reception. There are often no visible charts, record sheets or work instructions.

To make it worse, there is no definitive version of ISO 9000. Unlike Christianity, outsiders can't turn to a bible which will tell them what to do. There are, however, guidelines for some industries, which we examine in Appendix 3.

The language of the standard is very general. A typical clause runs as follows: 'A master list or equivalent document control procedure shall be established to identify the current revision of documents in order to preclude the use of non-applicable documents'. By the time you're half-way through this book, you will know what this is all about.

The authors of the Standard crafted it so carefully so that it would apply to all possible situations. This makes it a universal standard suitable for every kind of business. But it also means that the language is difficult to understand.

The media often criticises ISO 9000. Apart from its cost to small businesses, they attack its vagueness and complexity. Yet despite all these criticisms, more and more companies are seeking certification. Many people want to know more about the Standard. This book was written in response to that need. It aims to help you understand how ISO 9000 works, and what benefits it can bring.

A POTTED HISTORY OF THE STANDARD

Standards have been around a long time. For example, silver was first hallmarked in Britain in 1140 AD. But modern quality standards really developed in the 20th century, and they came from the military.

The military are obsessed with standardisation. If they make a change to one aeroplane, they carry out the same change to the whole fleet.

In pursuit of this standardisation, the US military produced a standard for quality control, which they wanted their civilian contractors to use. This was known as MIL STD 9858A, which is shown in Table 2.3.

This led to the Nato AQAP-1 Standard in 1968. The UK Ministry of Defence followed this with Def. Stan 05/21 in 1973.

But as late as the mid 1970s, there remained many different standards and documents. The military and major companies all issued their own standards for suppliers. Everyone agreed that it would be sensible to have one common standard for quality.

In 1974, the British Standards Institution introduced BS 5179, a guide to non-military quality assurance systems.

This led to BS 5750, which was first published in 1979. In its early form it was awarded to companies who had difficulty reaching the more stringent assessments that were later imposed.

Between 1979 and 1987, many other countries adopted similar quality standards. Many were identical copies of BS 5750.

This led to the International Organisation for Standardization (ISO) starting work in 1983 on an international standard.

The ISO standard was largely based on BS 5750, but it also reflected international requirements and eight years' experience by UK users.

The work was completed in 1987 with the publication of ISO 9000.

The ISO 9000 standards were then adopted in 1987 without deviation by Britain as the new BS 5750.

In Europe, CEN (the national standards organisations of 16 European countries) also adopted ISO 9000 as the European standard EN 29000: 1987.

Hence, in Britain, in Europe and throughout the world, the standard for quality management is identical. BS 5750, EN 29000, and ISO 9000 are all the same standard.

In 1994, minor revisions were made to the standard.

The Standard is a major international triumph. Around the world, most countries accept this standard, sometimes giving it their own name. It means that a manufacturer in Dusseldorf can order goods from a supplier in Dayton, Ohio, knowing that both companies are using parallel quality systems.

Companies trading in Britain tend to refer to the BS number. In Europe they refer to the EN, and outside Europe they refer to the ISO.

This leads to a confusing string of letters and numbers (such as references to BS 5750:Part 2/ISO 9002/EN 29002).

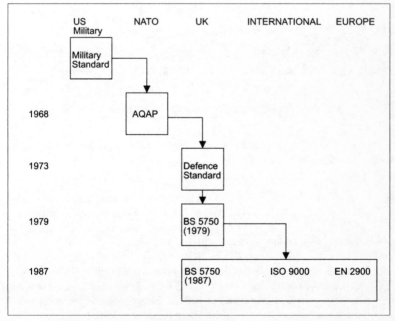

Table 2.3 The emergence of a single quality Standard

THE CONSTITUENT PARTS

ISO 9000 consists of two main parts, called ISO 9001 and ISO 9002.

ISO 9001 is the standard to adopt if your customers expect you to design and make products specially for them. For example, it would be suitable for an architect's practice. It is the more difficult of the two standards.

ISO 9002 is the standard for companies who make standardised goods, or whose customers don't ask them to design anything specially for them. It is a slightly easier standard.

Many manufacturing companies are certified to ISO 9002. Companies for whom design and development are important often go for the more advanced standard, ISO 9001. You can upgrade from ISO 9002 to ISO 9001.

As Table 2.4 shows, the two parts have different names in various parts of the world.

Table 2.4 Different names for the same standard

Three titles for the one group of standards			
Generic title	Main area of use	Standard for production and design	Standard for production
ISO 9000	USA, Pacific Rim	ISO 9001	ISO 9002
BS 5750	Britain	BS 5750 : Part 1	BS 5750 : Part 2
EN 29000	Europe	EN 29001	EN 29002

OTHER PARTS OF ISO 9000

If you're in a hurry, or you don't want to be confused with detail, you can go to the next box.

There are two guidance documents:

■ ISO 9000-1 (BS 5750 Section 0.1) helps you select the right part of the series. (Confusingly, it is similar to the title of the generic standard.)
■ ISO 9004 (BS 5750 Section 0.2) is a guide to overall quality management and the quality system elements.

There is also ISO 9003 (BS 5750 Part 3). This is for a company which wants to restrict itself to controlling quality through final inspection and test procedures. As a result it is a rather brief standard. ISO 9003 is not well used, being a rather old-fashioned approach to quality. In some countries, however, ISO 9003 is the base standard.

Chapter 5 helps you decide whether to go for ISO 9001 or ISO 9002.

HOW STANDARDS WON THE BATTLE OF WATERLOO

Most people know that the battle of Waterloo was an epic battle involving many European nations.

Fewer people know that British Standards were a decisive factor. The French cannons used different sizes of cannon ball. If your unit ran out of cannon balls, you were out of luck, because other units' cannon balls wouldn't fit.

The British, by contrast, had specified that all cannons and cannon balls had to have a standardised diameter. Any British ball could be used in any British cannon. This meant higher productivity, less wastage, less down-time, less cost, and less checking, to use 20th century language.

Learning the lesson from this, the British Standards Institution was set up just a few years later, the first of its type in the world. So if you are having difficulty with BS 5750, you can trace all your problems back to that historic battle.

ISO 9000 and software companies

If you produce or buy computer software, you'll need to know about Tickit. This is BS 5750 Part 1 (ISO 9001) as applied to software development. It applies to all kinds of software, whether off-the-shelf or tailor-made.

The use of poor quality software costs British industry £500 million a year, according to a report by Price Waterhouse for the Department of Trade and Industry (DTI). Another report (by CSC-Index for the DTI) says that 18 per cent of expenditure on computer systems is wasted. The report blames poor software as one element of this waste.

You can be certified to design, supply and maintain software, or to project manage it. You get your certificate from a certification body which is accredited for Tickit.

For an explanation of these terms, see Chapter 4 (Going for ISO 9000). See also Appendix 3.

ISO 9000 and stockists

Some companies simply buy stock and sell it to smaller companies or consumers. No processing takes place. This is the case for wholesalers, distributors, agents and retailers.

If your business fits this category, you need the ISO 9000 *stockist scheme*. By conforming to ISO 9000, you reassure customers that they will get consistent products and service. It will also help you improve your business.

You can ask BSI QA, BVQI and other certification bodies (listed in Appendix 3) for details of their stockist scheme.

SUMMARY

■ This book sets out to explain how ISO 9000 (BS 5750) works. (ISO 9000 and BS 5750 are the same standard.)

■ For ISO 9000, quality means 'fit for the purpose', not 'excellent'.

■ Quality assurance differs from quality control. QA is proactive and planned, and aims to build consistency into your process. QC merely attempts to pick out faulty goods out of a production line.

■ Adopting ISO 9000 (BS 5750) could make a big difference to the way you operate. Life should be more orderly, and the number of defective goods should decline.

■ With ISO 9000 you say what you're going to do, you do it, and then you prove you've done it.

■ It isn't easy. The language is complex and vague, and there is no defined way of implementing it.

■ BS 5750 was originally a military standard which civilian defence contractors had to obey. It was designed to ensure that aeroplanes stayed in the air, and that guns kept firing.

■ ISO 9000 sets out the outlines for a quality system. It's up to you to build a system that meets that outline.

■ If you produce software and you want ISO 9000, you will need the Tickit scheme. If you are a wholesaler or retailer, you will need a stockist scheme.

SEPARATING FACT FROM FICTION

◆

In this chapter you'll discover:

- ■ Five complaints people make about ISO 9000.
- ■ Six myths about ISO 9000.
- ■ The real advantages and disadvantages of ISO 9000.

FIVE COMPLAINTS ABOUT ISO 9000

There are many myths and misconceptions about ISO 9000. You need to understand what the standard can and can't do for your organisation. Here are five of the main complaints that people make about ISO 9000.

First complaint: I've heard you can produce rubbish and still get ISO 9000

This is technically true. You can specify low grade goods in your manual. As long as you produce goods no worse than your plan, you can get ISO 9000.

In practice it would be difficult, even perverse, to set up all the planning, inspection and testing that ISO 9000 requires, and still produce really low grade products.

ISO 9000 aims to help you produce consistent products. Using ISO 9000, you're less likely to produce defective products.

Let's imagine you make cheap plastic toys for Christmas crackers. A precision engineering company might think your toys were crudely made. But your customer, the cracker manufacturer, will be delighted because he can buy inexpensive little items. And children (his customers) will be thrilled to get a free toy in their cracker.

If, however, one in ten of your novelties is an unrecognisable charred blob, then the manufacturer and the child will get cross. They will rightly say that your products aren't fit for their purpose.

Second complaint: We've been producing quality goods for years. We don't need a badge to prove it.

Some companies feel cornered. Having produced high grade products for decades, they see new businesses in their market place flaunting their ISO 9000 certificates.

These old-established companies have loyal customers and dedicated staff. They don't have anything to prove. But the very existence of ISO 9000 makes them feel uneasy.

If you're in this position, look at the lists of benefits listed later in the chapter. See if any of them are relevant to you.

ISO 9000 is one of the few ways you can *prove* you produce consistent products. If you don't have the certificate, why should anyone believe you? It's only your word, after all.

ISO 9000 won't work for everyone. But not having the badge can makes companies feel inadequate. You can hear customers asking, 'If your production is so excellent, why haven't you got ISO 9000? Why don't you apply for it? What have you got to lose?' These are cruel questions. But they illustrate the dilemma that some companies face.

Remember, too, that standards are getting higher, and competition is getting tougher. What was acceptable in the market place a few years ago may no longer be acceptable. A customer who buys from you when you are the main supplier might switch to a newcomer if that company offers proof of quality through ISO 9000.

Third complaint: I've got a quality system in place that meets the requirements of ISO 9000. I don't need certification.

This is true for many companies. They have good systems in place. And they don't feel like paying a certification body to prove it.

But a check by an independent outside organisation is bound to be more rigorous than your own, perhaps tolerant, review. It's why students can't mark their own essays and why, in ISO 9000, staff can't audit their own work.

Independent verification is common in many areas of life. You can't drive a car until you have been tested.

The independent check also gives you useful information. It tells you whether your system truly matches the standard. It tells you whether there are gaps in your system, ones which might allow product faults to slip through.

Other external audits are done by quality consultants with experience of scrutinising hundreds of companies – they probably know a lot more about how to prevent quality failures than you do. So it is worth asking their views, and heeding their advice. It could help to improve your business.

To keep your registration, you have to undergo an external assessment twice a year. This prevents you from getting complacent, and letting your standards slip. Like Christianity, you never know when to expect a call.

Fourth complaint: paying for certification will be expensive.

Small firms find certification expensive. It can cost several thousand pounds in the first year. But some certification bodies allow you to spread the payments over three years. And others have schemes for small businesses which involve fewer visits and therefore lower costs.

Apart from the cost of certification, there should not be any other costs. Wise companies make do with existing staff and introduce a streamlined system.

If, however, you hire a management consultancy, there will be fees to pay. But as we see later, there are ways of keeping these costs down.

SGS Yarsley, a certification body, reports that 'On average, payback from ISO 9000 is achieved under three years'. Some have achieved payback much faster, and some companies' profits soar after introducing ISO 9000.

If you lose a big customer by not having ISO 9000 or because you sold him faulty products, the cost of the lost business will outweigh the costs of getting ISO 9000.

Fifth complaint: our customers buy what is cheapest. So we couldn't increase our costs or our quality.

ISO 9000 doesn't set out special requirements which only a few firms can – or need – comply with. It is a practical standard that can be used by all companies. ISO 9000 could actually help you cut your costs.

What's more, customers are increasingly looking for long term relationships with their suppliers. They expect their suppliers to provide consistent goods, at the lowest cost – and to be certified to ISO 9000.

Case history: Poor quality goods from a ISO 9000 company

A decorative laminate factory (let's call it A) was certified to ISO 9000.

When it got too busy, it asked another ISO 9000 company (we'll call it B) to fulfil the orders.

A's production manager was cross when he saw B's work. 'This is nowhere near our quality' he said, 'and it's going out in our name.' He pointed out that the joints were neither straight nor properly glued.

The Managing Director knew a third firm (C). It wasn't registered to ISO 9000. In order to check its quality, he sent one of his most skilled carpenters to assess it.

The carpenter duly reported that he was impressed with C's work, which was of a high standard. So his company passed its overflow work to the new company.

The story might have a happy ending. It might have proved that ISO 9000 is no guarantee of excellence.

Actually, the new supplier produced work that was even worse than B. This was because it was skilled at carpentry, but had little experience of laminate.

The real moral is that you should understand the strengths and weaknesses of your suppliers (something that ISO 9000 covers, as we'll see in Chapter 7).

SIX MYTHS ABOUT ISO 9000

Myth 1: Once you've got ISO 9000, you can only buy from other ISO 9000 companies.

Not true. The standard simply says that you should keep a record of acceptable suppliers. It is up to you to define what makes them acceptable. Your previous experience of them will be a major consideration.

Equally, there is nothing to stop you writing in your quality manual that you will only buy from ISO 9000 registered suppliers. But that would be a hostage to fortune.

Myth 2: ISO 9000 is only for big companies.

More and more small firms are deciding to go for ISO 9000. This is often because their customers expect them to have it. For them, ISO 9000 is the price of staying in business.

One such organisation is Halton General Hospital's Electro-Bio Medical Engineering Unit. It has only three members of staff.

The unit was keen to get ISO 9000 because it was seeking work outside the hospital. Many of its health service customers were becoming more commercially minded, and were themselves getting ISO 9000. The medical engineering unit wanted to keep this work and get more of it.

Myth 3: It produces lots of paper.

You already have much of the paperwork required by ISO 9000. You probably have purchase orders, drawings and various records. ISO 9000 simply brings them all together into a coherent system.

ISO 9000 can even cut the paperwork. When it implemented the Standard, an ambulance service reduced the number of forms from 270 to 78.

If you haven't got written procedures that specify how work should be carried out, maybe you should. You might find that staff don't do what you think they do. You might also find that staff are unsure about what they are supposed to do.

A client once criticised the organisation I worked for. We had produced reports on 12 of his sites. The trouble was, the reports were in three different styles. There was no consistency about them. He guessed that they had been produced by three different people, each with their own idea of what ought to be in the report. There was no standardised method of report writing, and this led to client dissatisfaction.

Myth 4: It requires lots of extra staff.

A large firm will need a quality manager (possibly appointed from within the business); a smaller business might give the work on a part-time basis to an existing employee.

Therefore, there is no reason why you should need any more staff. In fact, extra staff could be a sign that your quality system is not working properly.

ISO 9000 could even help you reduce staff. Many companies find that once their system is working, it cuts out re-work and errors. As a result, the company needs fewer staff. This is a surprisingly common experience.

You could adopt a policy of 'no extra staff' for the quality system. This will ensure that you create a slimline system. Staff can inspect their own work and audit others' work providing they weren't directly involved with it. So there should be no need for extra inspectors or auditors.

Myth 5: It's only for manufacturers.

ISO 9000 was developed to meet the needs of manufacturers. So if you have an engineering business, it will be perfect for your needs.

If you work in a service organisation, you'll find it more challenging. Construction companies also find it a challenge, because they don't have a fixed product.

Unfortunately, there isn't an international standard for service companies (thought there is a guideline). But all kinds of service companies have found that ISO 9000 meets their needs.

Some service companies have an intangible product (such as a nursing home). Others have more tangible products (a restaurant serves meals). But wherever you have staff, things are likely to go wrong. Nursing home staff can give old people the wrong medication. In fast food restaurants, staff can burn the hamburgers or operate the till wrongly.

ISO 9000 is just as good at helping a hotel manage its laundry, bars and reception desk as it is helping a defence contractor produce its tanks on time.

Myth 6. ISO 9000 would force us to adopt a specific level of quality – perhaps lower than we already have.

ISO 9000 doesn't set any particular level of quality. That is done by you and your customers. ISO 9000 merely requires that you have systems in place which maintain your quality at a pre-determined level, one that is set by you.

With ISO 9000, you state how you intend to carry out your production process. And you keep records showing that you did what you planned to do.

Every human being has the same skeleton but our bodies all look different. It's the same with ISO 9000. The Standard is a skeleton on which you build your own quality system.

THE REAL ADVANTAGES AND DISADVANTAGES OF ISO 9000

Having looked at the complaints and myths, what are the real advantages and drawbacks of ISO 9000? That is the next topic we consider. Table 3.1 summarises some of the main benefits. This is followed by a more detailed look at some of the points.

Table 3.1 The advantages of ISO 9000

ADVANTAGES OF ISO 9000	
For your employees	
1.	Staff get a better understanding of their role and objectives, by having a documented management system.

2.	They benefit from reduced stress levels, because they are using an efficient management system, and because they know what is expected of them.
3.	They get increased morale and a sense of pride through achieving the goals of registration and customer satisfaction
4.	New staff can immediately learn their job, because the details are in writing.

For your organisation

1.	Your products will be of a more consistent quality, and you will produce fewer rejects.
2.	You gain cost savings, because your production will be more efficient. There are economies in production (because your systems are controlled from start to finish), and economies in time that was formerly spent re-doing work.
3.	You can improve the quality of your raw materials by requiring your suppliers to have a ISO 9000 system.
4.	Export marketing is easier, because some foreign buyers recognise ISO 9000 (BS 5750).
5.	You can expect preferential treatment from potential customers who have ISO 9000 certification. This means an increase in new business.
6.	You secure greater customer loyalty, because you continuously satisfy their needs and give them no cause to seek another supplier. That means you suffer fewer customer losses.
7.	You can use ISO 9000 in your publicity to win more sales.
8.	ISO 9000 helps you minimise the risk of producing unsafe products. It may also give you some protection in law against product liability claims.
9.	Being first in your area or industry may put you ahead of your rivals by 18 months to two years.

For your customers

1.	Your customers get a known level of quality that is independently audited.
2.	They get a means of choosing between competing suppliers.
3.	They can have more confidence in your goods.

4.	ISO 9000 minimises their risk, by pushing responsibility on to their supplier (ie you).
5.	They can manage you, their supplier, better by specifying that you must have a ISO 9000 system.
6.	They can assess your quality system, and thus check your ability to produce satisfactory goods and services.

Financial benefits

A survey by SGS Yarsley asked companies who had ISO 9000 to list areas where major cost savings were identified. 27 per cent said they had fewer rejects, 20 per cent reduced administration, 20 per cent increased productivity, 18 per cent removed unnecessary procedures, and 15 per cent achieved savings in overtime payments.

The costs of poor quality may be higher than you think. The average 'cost of quality' is between 5 per cent and 25 per cent of a company's turnover according to government figures.

There are the wages of your quality inspectors, the cost of scrap, and the wages of operators doing re-work. There are the costs of extra deliveries (perhaps using express delivery), the lost production, and the cost of senior people's time. You can also add the cost of business lost due to customer dissatisfaction.

Thus ISO 9000 becomes a matter of urgency rather than a useful management project.

Doubling your profit

Reducing your cost of quality could transfer an unexpected fortune to your profits. Let's say you make 10 per cent profit on sales. If you can reduce the cost of quality from 20 per cent to 10 per cent, *you double your profits*.

Think for a moment of your sales people, struggling to maintain sales. Think of the sheer impossibility of doubling your sales in a competitive market. Think of your Financial Director trying to hold up his margin. Yet potentially you could double your profit by reducing your quality errors.

Increased effectiveness

The Managing Partner of a law firm which gained ISO 9000 said, 'ISO 9000 helps generate a culture of responsiveness. As well as being disciplined about replying to letters and phone calls, ISO 9000 also requires the setting up of a formal complaints system'.

He went on: 'It means that the company no longer sits on complaints from customers; the system is able to identify where things are going wrong at an early stage. It underpins the culture of partnership which should be about sharing difficulties, not concealing them'.

Satisfying customer's requirements

Today, more corporate customers require their suppliers to have ISO 9000.

Even service companies and not-for-profit organisations are finding that government agencies and funding bodies are increasingly asking if they have ISO 9000. The reason is simple: all purchasers have to justify their expenditure.

Things can and do go wrong, and organisations need to protect themselves against risk. If anything goes wrong, shareholders may question whether the money was spent wisely. The purchaser can say, 'We checked them out. They had ISO 9000'.

Many companies go for ISO 9000 because their big corporate customers expect it. But if you get ISO 9000 just to satisfy a big customer, you miss out on a lot.

A company whose only aim is to have a certificate for its reception wall will never discover the real benefits of ISO 9000.

Many companies start out like this, and get converted on the way. They grudgingly come to recognise the benefits of ISO 9000, and many of them end up as devotees. This happens because they find out that ISO 9000 gives them more advantages than they were expecting.

Easier growth

When reviewing itself, one charity found that it had grown substantially since it was founded in 1970. While communication and co-ordination are easy in a small organisation, they become more difficult as the organisation grows. This is especially true if your organisation has more than one site.

The same applied to a construction firm. It opened new offices in several cities, and found that ISO 9000 helped to harmonise systems across its different sites. It also found that staff who had come from other construction companies used different methods. ISO 9000 was able to provide a definitive method.

Case history: the tile maker who got ISO 9000 for the wrong reasons

A hand-made roof tile company openly admitted that it had acquired ISO 9000 just so that the company could get on to architects' tender lists.

It was clear that the quality culture was not very deep in this company.

The managing director had the jobs of quality manager and marketing director. As far as he was concerned, he had achieved his objective. He was now getting tenders for work which, without ISO 9000, he wouldn't have got.

But if the company is not committed to ISO 9000, and fails to maintain its system, the company might lose its certification. Moreover, the company will not benefit from any of the improvements which a serious implementation of ISO 9000 can bring.

Looking more professional

People expect professionalism these days, even from not-for-profit organisations. The days are gone when you could justify sloppy performance by claiming that you are a creative organisation, a voluntary group, or concerned with people's welfare.

To survive and compete in your arena, you have to look your best, and ISO 9000 can help you do that.

It can help you get the CE Mark

The CE mark is a product standard, which is associated with ISO 9000. It is a kind of passport which allows your goods to cross European countries.

It is a declaration to market inspectors throughout the EC that your product complies with the relevant EC directives.

There are now many such directives. Some relate to specific products – for example, toys. Others are wide ranging, covering the safety of industrial machinery.

Products covered by the directives cannot be sold in EC countries unless they carry out the mark. Failure to comply with the legislation is a criminal offence.

You can get the CE mark through a number of different processes. They include having your product independently tested and by having the ISO 9000 standard.

The net effect of this legislation will be to increase the number of firms in Europe and throughout the world who need ISO 9000.

Other trading blocks are also developing product standards like the CE mark. These, too, are likely to be based on ISO 9000.

Table 3.2 Before and after the introduction of ISO 9000

THE EFFECTS OF ISO 9000	
Before	**After**
Knowledge about work processes is stored in people's minds. It is often out of date or wrong	Work processes are written down, and everyone works to the same procedures
Production staff are concerned to 'push the product out of the door'	Production staff are concerned to 'get it right'
Quality is seen as the responsibility of QC inspectors	Quality is seen as everyone's responsibility
Substantial re-work and scrap	Little scrap and re-work
Complaints from customers	Few complaints
Large hidden costs constrain the company	The business is more profitable

THE DISADVANTAGES OF ISO 9000

There are various problems associated with ISO 9000. We look at these next.

Cost

ISO 9000 is going to cost you money. There is the cost of the initial assessment and certification, surveillance costs, the costs of extra meetings and planning, and the costs of extra checking.

People who believe in ISO 9000 say that these costs will be offset by the savings and efficiencies achieved by the standard. But there are still costs for which cheques have to be written.

Staff

In nominating a quality manager, you will take someone away from their existing duties. Or you may hire an extra member of staff. Either of these options is expensive.

Time

You can't get ISO 9000 overnight. It takes between six months and two years to reach certification. During that time, you could have been progressing other projects.

Effort

For any organisation, ISO 9000 requires a lot of work. People are going to have to struggle to write procedures and to undergo training.

Change

Members of staff may resent the changes that you are introducing. Some may leave. Others may be obstructive.

The possibility of failure

Not every implementation works. Some businesses say that ISO 9000 brought them no benefits.

Defenders of ISO 9000 would say that no quality programme will of itself turn around a company which is not profitable, or whose products are not wanted.

Often companies approach a quality programme for the wrong reasons. A survey of the quality programmes of America's top 1,000 corporations suggests that 'most companies were forced to join the quality revolution [not for altruistic reasons, but], due to a crisis within their industry or company'.

Below, we look at some of the problems that a bad implementation of ISO 9000 can bring.

Bureaucracy

ISO 9000 often features large manuals. Some are said to be so large that they have to be fitted with wheels to be moved around.

There can be a proliferation of quality staff. More manuals, more paperwork, more meetings, more measurements. The real aspects of quality are overlooked.

I was meeting the works director of an engineering firm when the internal mail arrived. The messenger put a large manual on his desk. It was titled *Corporate environmental manual*.

He picked it up – with both hands – and put it with a sigh on a shelf beside other hefty volumes. They were labelled *Corporate quality manual*, *Corporate style manual*, and *Corporate purchasing manual*.

Had he ever read any of these manuals, I asked? No, he hadn't. They were just too much effort.

If you're a bureaucratic company, you'll introduce a bureaucratic system. It's up to you to prove you are a smart business by developing a slimline quality system.

Companies that complain about ISO 9000 are really complaining about the way they implemented it, not the standard itself. If you have a bureaucratic system, prune it.

Excessive numbers of procedures

Tom Peters, who wrote *The Pursuit of Excellence*, says: 'Some companies even have procedures to tell their workforce when to go to the lavatory'.

In other words, he feels that people should be empowered or entrusted to do the work.

You have to guard against writing procedures for the sake of it. Maybe you should institute a purge of irrelevant procedures every 12 months.

Inflexibility

Some companies design systems that are inflexible and unwieldy. That is the wrong attitude.

ISO 9000 should help you grow, not restrict you. For example, a food processor obtained ISO 9000 for its new product development department. It wanted to ensure that the department operated professionally, to increase the new products' chances of success.

Case history: the buyer's perspective

Sandra works for an organisation that trains nurses.

'When sales reps try to sell us something,' she says, 'they say, "We've got ISO 9000".'

'When I ask them what that means,' she says, 'they don't seem to know. It's as though they believe ISO 9000 entitles them to get the order. They don't really consider what benefit it brings us.'

She went on: 'I don't see any real difference in quality between companies which have the standard and those which don't. For instance, we have an excellent printer who doesn't have the standard'.

'I ask companies, "If you were to get the contract, how would you fulfil it? What steps would you take to do the work?" I'm impressed by companies which seem to know what they are doing.'

But Sandra admits that ISO 9000 plays an important role in selecting suppliers. 'When we have a tender-opening session, we check to see who has a low price and ISO 9000. Companies which have both go forward to the short list.'

SUMMARY

- ISO 9000 is not a guarantee of excellence, merely of consistency. Some companies with ISO 9000 have low standards.
- Some companies install a ISO 9000 system but don't have it independently assessed. This means they lose a competitive advantage.
- Some companies believe that customers only buy cheapest. Today, suppliers want a long term relationship. At the very least they want suppliers who are both cheap and have ISO 9000.
- ISO 9000 is for all kinds of organisations, big and small, manufacturing and service.
- ISO 9000 does not set a particular level of quality. Your customers do that.
- ISO 9000 should not increase your numbers of staff. It might even allow you to reduce the numbers. It should give you cost savings and increased customer satisfaction.
- But ISO 9000 also has disadvantages. They include the cost of certification, the time it takes, and the disruption to the business.
- Companies who implement it badly can suffer from bureaucracy, an excessive number of procedures, and inflexibility.

GOING FOR ISO 9000

◆

In this chapter, you'll learn about:

- ■ The organisations you'll meet.
- ■ Appointing a quality manager.
- ■ Getting staff commitment.
- ■ Writing a policy.
- ■ Writing procedures and auditing the system.
- ■ Getting registered.

THE ORGANISATIONS YOU WILL MEET

Let's imagine that your company decides to go for ISO 9000 (BS 5750). As Figure 4.1 shows, you start implementing the system, possibly with the help of a management consultancy (whose involvement we consider in the next chapter).

Then you apply for registration to a certification body, of which there are many. This organisation visits your plant. It checks your documentation and your actual practices.

If your system meets the requirements of ISO 9000, you are given the award – certification to ISO 9000. To maintain certification, you will receive unannounced 'surveillance' visits two times a year from the same certification body.

Accreditation bodies

The best certification bodies have, in turn, been checked by a national accreditation body to make sure that they are competent to certify companies. This accreditation body is appointed by the government or a similar official body. In the UK, accreditation is provided by the National Accreditation Council for Certification Bodies (NACCB).

NACCB verifies that the certification company is independent, impartial, competent and knowledgeable. It also checks that the company uses qualified and experienced staff, and is thorough in its assessments.

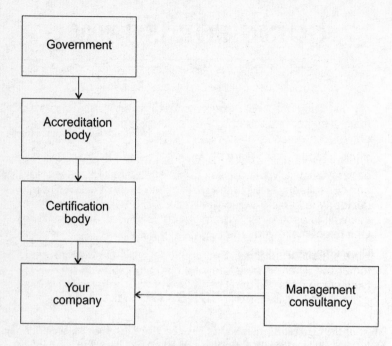

Figure 4.1 How ISO9000 works

You are unlikely to have any dealings with NACCB, because it doesn't normally get involved with the certification of individual companies.

What are certification bodies?

Certification bodies exist to certify companies to ISO 9000 and other standards. They make their money by charging you for assessment and surveillance visits.

Many people treat them with enormous respect, even reverence. They don't realise that many certification bodies are simply profit-making businesses, no different in outlook from a furniture manufacturer or a bank.

Some of them have consultancy operations. So although one part is only concerned with assessment, another wants to sell you consultancy services. It is by no means unusual to find the certification body telling you that in addition to paying its normal fees, you should also pay for a 'pre-assessment visit'.

An unscrupulous organisation will even emphasise that you have a higher chance of getting certification if you go through one of its pre-assessment visits.

There is something called a 'Chinese wall' (in other words a paper wall) which is supposed to exist between the assessment and consultancy arms of the certification body. It is up to you to decide whether the two organisations are whispering through this wall to each other. You might decide this is an advantage. Or it might make you cross.

Here's another surprise. You could set up a certification body tomorrow. There is absolutely nothing stopping you from certifying companies. So don't be in awe of your certification body.

Most of the big certification bodies have been approved by an accreditation body (see above), which acts as a watchdog. So if you are talking to a certification body, check whether it has received accreditation. As time goes by, the numbers of certification bodies will grow. New, specialised certification bodies will sprout, some offering you apparent expertise in your industry. Look before you leap.

IMPLEMENTING THE SYSTEM

It's time to act. You've decided to go for ISO 9000 (BS 5750). So you need to get people working towards registration. The tasks are summarised in Figure 4.2. At some point you have to decide whether to choose ISO 9001 or ISO 9002. That is something we consider in the next chapter. In the meantime, the steps to take are as follows.

Appoint a quality manager

Most companies appoint a quality manager or, in smaller companies, a quality controller. In a small firm, the executive will have a 'proper' job besides managing the system, while in a larger company the task will be full-time.

On matters of quality, the manager should report directly to a board

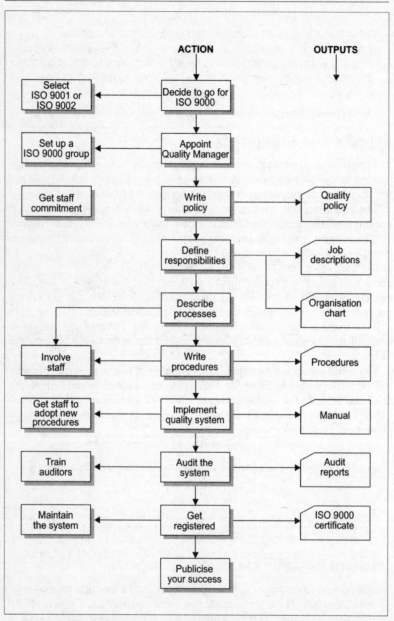

Figure 4.2 The steps towards ISO 9000

member. If you value quality, you must give your manager the ability to get things changed. That means having access to the boss.

It is also desirable to separate the manager from the production department. Being part of the production department will mean that the quality manager will come under intolerable pressure to accept lower standards of quality. That is why many organisation charts show the quality department in a little box on its own, with a line straight to the Chief Executive.

Set up a ISO 9000 group

The quality manager can't implement ISO 9000 by himself. For one thing, it is too big a job to create the system on his own. For another, only the workforce can maintain the records and do the daily checks.

The last thing you want to do is to hand your managers a ready-made system. It will be seen as an alien invention, imposed on them from outside.

What's more, you lose a valuable benefit of ISO 9000. In order to write procedures, managers have to analyse the way things are done. During this phase, they often find better ways to do the work. If you write the procedures yourself, or get consultants to do it for you, that benefit is lost. The manager who said to me, 'I'll get these procedures written and sent to all the staff' hadn't really understood the benefits of delegation.

Even worse is the seagull school of management. Here a large manual is dropped from a great height, with the seagull last seen flying off into the distance.

You could set up a committee. The managers of all the departments who will be affected should be on it. The committee should be chaired by the chief executive or the quality manager could call a meeting.

Set a date for the committee to be dissolved. It does not need to be a permanent part of your business.

Case history: the chemical company whose system doesn't work.

'Our ISO 9000 is a millstone,' says the newly appointed quality manager of a small detergent and disinfectant chemical company. 'Its 90 employees,' he says, 'have little awareness of what the system does.'

'Communication is poor,' he says. 'The staff think that the system is used to control them. They ask why we do it. They don't see the big picture. There is no training, no explanation of benefits.'

'When the workforce is about to be audited, the staff say, "The auditors are coming – how far out of shape are we?" They pay lip service to the standard.'

'We need a culture change,' he says. 'It must be from the top down. The staff must be helped to understand. We must explain what the standard is for.'

Get staff commitment

It is important to get the chief executive's commitment to the project. If staff see that he wants ISO 9000, and that he attends the project meetings, they will work to make it a success. If they see that he has only lukewarm enthusiasm, or doesn't believe in it, they won't make the effort.

It is also important to motivate managers and staff. You can do this by explaining to them the purpose of the system and the benefits they will get.

Your attitude towards the managers is important. If you behave in an overbearing way, insisting that they conform to the new system, they will respond negatively.

'Call the Standard "ISO 8999",' said one PR manager. 'It will be one number short – and that's me, because I'm not getting involved.' The manager was being humorous, but her words indicated her underlying fears.

There are many ways that staff can sabotage the system. They can criticise the standard to their subordinates, ensuring its instant failure. They will tell everyone that the standard isn't suitable for the business. Then they will make the prophecy come true. They do this by failing to write procedures. They will ignore the procedures in practice, doing work in quite different ways. And they will fail to keep records. This will ensure that you never gain certification.

For more on staff involvement and motivation, see Chapter 9.

Write a quality policy

In its opening words, ISO 9000 asks you to produce a quality policy. This is usually a one page document, which commits the company to quality by means of ISO 9000. A typical example is shown below.

The problem with all kinds of company statements is that they are often ignored. A typical workforce prefers to judge management by what it practises, not by what it preaches.

The one advantage of the quality policy as defined by ISO 9000 (BS 5750) is that it is usually signed by 'management'. This normally means the highest executive. Having put his name to it, the Chief Executive will usually be keen to see that it is followed through.

QUALITY POLICY

It is the policy of XYZ Ltd to continually meet and exceed customers' needs profitably. This is the only way to ensure the company's future prosperity.

To this end, the company has instituted a quality system which complies with ISO 9002.

All staff shall be familiar with the quality procedures which are relevant to their work, and shall comply with them.

Signed   A ANDREWS
                            Chief Executive

The policy is also a useful document for demonstrating the company's commitment to quality – both to staff and to customers.

The standard requires the policy to be understood throughout the organisation. This means ensuring that the workforce know what procedures apply to them, and how they are supposed to use them. This is a major step forward for many companies.

Define responsibilities

One of ISO 9000's main roles is to clarify responsibilities, a subject that we examine in more detail in Chapter 9.

You may work for an organisation in which everyone knows their job, and lines of authority are clearly defined. If so, you are fortunate. In many companies, people have several bosses, they don't know exactly what is expected of them, and the lines of communication are uncertain.

Solving these problems reduces the likelihood of error, because it reduces uncertainty. It also improves motivation, and this is one of the many unexpected benefits that ISO 9000 (BS 5750) can bring.

Describe how your company's processes work

Every organisation has a core process. The chemical company mentioned in the case history above buys chemicals, mixes them in large vats, and sells them in 25 litre containers.

Some companies have a string of processes. A builder finds land, gets planning permission, designs buildings, gets a sub-contractor to erect the buildings, and then sells them.

A unit trust company designs a financial service, advertises for investors, invests the money, and pays back investors.

Errors can creep into all these processes. The chemical company can mix the wrong chemicals. The construction company can design houses that no one wants to buy. The unit trust can buy the wrong investments.

You can reduce the number of errors by having written procedures. The chemical company should have a written recipe. The construction company should check its new building designs against those that are proven in the market. The unit trust company can have procedures that reduce the risk in buying shares.

ISO 9000 expects you to manage your core process properly, by having written procedures for it. We examine this in more detail in Chapter 6. But to continue our review of Figure 4.2, it is worth looking at how to write the procedures.

Write the procedures

This job should be undertaken at the level at which the work is carried out. If you don't think your supervisors or operatives are capable of doing the work, you probably underestimate them. They will need a standard format, and you will have to show them how to write a procedure. But get them to do the work wherever possible. What's more, dividing the work as thinly as possible avoids an overload of work for people who are probably already overworked.

Be as flexible as possible. Fit in with the needs of the staff (in terms of their timing, venue and preferred ways of working). This will limit the time involved, minimise the disruption, and stop them feeling that they are being imposed upon.

Use this opportunity to reflect on what you are doing. Are you doing it the best way? Try to make improvements wherever you can. This will help people realise that the procedures are not tablets of stone. Rather, they are messages on blackboards, which can be altered. The quality manager can act as 'devil's advocate' at this point, asking people whether the way they do things is genuinely the best way.

Written procedures help a company get control over its process. A Phillips factory which made specialised parts for television sets asked consultants to examine a production problem. The Technical Manager brought out work instructions for that process. The consultants could quickly get to the heart of the problem because it had been accurately written down (or documented, to use ISO 9000 language).

Implement the quality system

Now is the time to gather all your procedures into a manual. You now have an ISO 9000 system in operation!

You'll have to ensure that all staff are actually following the procedures. If you have involved them, and written down what is best practice, the staff should be using the proper procedures.

Case history: Building firm sorts out its paperwork.

'Paperwork has decreased, not increased, since we installed ISO 9000,' says Nick Kingsman, Director of Denne Builders.

'We now issue one 12-page document at the start of each building project which outlines every aspect from tender to handover.'

Formalising procedures at the very beginning of a project cuts out extraneous paperwork while ensuring that nothing is left out. Site staff also know in advance exactly what needs to be done at every project stage.

It was the potential threat of losing customers that made Denne Builders consider ISO 9000 in the first place. Now the quality standard is helping the company win new business. 'We are now on many bidding lists,' says Nick Kingsman, 'because we are able to tick the appropriate boxes on the pre-qualification documents.'

Audit the system

In Chapter 11 we look at how to carry out audits. Your chosen certification body will look for evidence that you are carrying out regular audits of the system.

But more importantly, the audits are your eyes and ears. They will tell you where your quality is failing, and give you the opportunity to improve.

At this point, you should be looking for errors in the system, and correcting them.

Get registered

You need to put thought into choosing a certification body. The criteria are as follows:

- Is it accredited? (See 'Accreditation bodies', above).
- How much prestige does it have?
- Does it operate internationally? Do your export customers know of it?
- Do its staff understand your industry?
- How do its charges compare with other certification bodies?
- How flexible is it likely to be when it comes to little errors in your system?

In Chapter 13 we look in more detail about selecting a certification body.

Publicise your success

After all your hard work, you're entitled to promote your certificate. Make sure all your customers know. We look at this in Chapter 14.

CREATING A PLAN

In the last few pages we have covered many topics. It is worth considering the important issues in putting together a quality system. Prime among those is having a plan, as we see next.

You need to plan how you will achieve ISO 9000. Few companies can implement it in less than a year. Some companies take two years. A small, smart organisation might succeed in six months if it knows what it is doing, and is dedicated to achieving it.

Realistic timescales must be set. Staff must be allocated time to do the work. If you expect a production manager to develop ISO 9000 in his spare time, you need not be surprised that the project takes years to implement.

You should set out the main milestones, and the dates by which you will have achieved them. This will give you a set of targets. Nothing concentrates the mind better than knowing that you are about to be audited in four weeks' time.

Then there is the question of people. Like any initiative, ISO 9000 must be fully endorsed by top management. Also, the staff need to be properly introduced to ISO 9000. They may feel threatened by the standard if they don't understand it. It is vital to explain the advantages of ISO 9000, and how it can help them do their job better.

Try to get the design right. Ensure that your system is as small and neat as possible. Avoid huge manuals that contain unnecessary detail – they will weigh your company down.

STARTING A BENCHMARK

Before you take any action, take some measurements. They will be your benchmark. Start a chart showing a key indicator. Do this before people start to change the way they do things.

What should you measure? Look for the things that demonstrate a failure of quality. It might be the number of complaints, the percentage of work that fails inspection, or the number of returns from customers. Try and cost them if you can.

In a year's time, you will be able to judge the effect of ISO 9000. If the key indicator has not moved, you have a problem. Maybe the workforce has ignored ISO 9000, and gone on as if nothing had happened?

Maybe you always had an excellent product. Or maybe you have a process that doesn't respond to the disciplines of ISO 9000. In practice, this situation is rare.

It is more likely that you will initially see an increase in faults. As people's awareness of quality improves, they are more likely to take faulty goods off the line instead of letting them continue.

But as the months go by, you should see a downward trend in the number of faults. This shows you have moved to a higher level of quality. By the end of the twelve months, you should be able to put value on the savings that ISO 9000 has brought, by adding up the cumulative reduction in quality failures.

Some benefits may not be readily apparent, such as the financial benefit of retaining a customer or winning new ones. Your sales department will put this down to their excellent salesmanship,but you will know better.

SUMMARY

- Certification bodies exist to assess companies. They are regulated by an accreditation body. A third organisation is the management consultancy, which you might use to help you implement ISO 9000.
- You will need to appoint a quality manager. Make sure he reports directly to a board member. Make sure he does not report to production.
- The quality manager's job is to supervise the quality system – he is not a glorified inspector.
- You will need to set up an ISO 9000 committee, consisting of line managers, the chief executive and quality manager. The committee's task is to decide how to create the quality system.
- Write a quality policy.
- Draw up an organisation chart, and provide job descriptions for key staff.
- Make sure all staff know what is going on, and why you are introducing ISO 9000.
- Make line management write the procedures. This is the only way to make sure they are involved.
- Audit your new system.

- Appoint a certification body, and have it assess your system. Once you pass, publicise your success.
- Establish a benchmark for making comparisons later.

THE RIGHT APPROACH

◆

In this chapter, you'll learn about:

■ Certifying the right part of your business.
■ Which departments to choose.
■ Which part of the standard to apply for.
■ Whether to use a consultancy.

CERTIFYING THE RIGHT PART OF YOUR BUSINESS

Some companies want to certify their entire organisation at one go. Others want to approach ISO 9000 (BS 5750) more cautiously, and seek certification for one division at a time.

If your organisation is small, the decision is easy. If you have just one small compact site and one simple product, you will apply to have the one site certified.

But what if you have several plants in the same town? What if you have branches all over the country? What if you are vertically integrated, and you undertake all kinds of different processes?

Complex companies have more difficulty deciding whether to certify all of their business, or just a part of it. They may be unsure whether to start with a relatively unimportant part of the business, and evaluate its success. Or they may decide to certify the core business.

There are no quick answer to these questions, because each company is different. But there are a few issues that apply to any project.

■ Don't undertake a project that you can't manage. Too large an exercise may get out of hand. Do you have a region or division that could start the process?
■ Decide what the most important factors are. Are you worried by complaints about products from one particular plant?
■ Is one part of the business crucial to the organisation's future? Are some of your businesses less significant? Should you go for the most important part of your company? Or are you worried that ISO 9000 might cause disruption, even permanent damage?

■ Are some businesses run as separate profit centres? If so, should the management be asked to decide for themselves?

■ Do you have an ISO 9000 champion in one of the departments? Is he keen to implement the standard, and could his enthusiasm lead the staff?

■ Do you have a branch network? If so, should you select some branches to undertake a pilot exercise first? Perhaps the others could benefit from the mistakes and problems encountered in the pilot exercise?

WHICH DEPARTMENTS TO CHOOSE

This leads to the question – which departments should you certify? In the past, a manufacturing organisation would include only the production, design, purchasing and warehouse departments. These are the departments that clearly affect the quality of the product.

For a service organisation, selecting the right departments is more complex. The production department might be the organisation's architects, planners, consultants or telephonists.

In a manufacturing or service business, branch management or van drivers could also affect quality.

Some businesses place all their departments under an ISO 9000 regime. And why not? It puts everyone on a level footing. Everyone contributes to the organisation's success. And under ISO 9000 everyone will be working to the same system. So consider including more than just narrowly defined production people. Only you can decide which departments are relevant.

Imagine that you get slow or inadequate financial information from your finance department. With ISO 9000, you could write instructions for the department specifying what information will be provided and when. The quality audits of your quality system would then regularly check to see whether the department was doing this.

If sales and marketing are part of the quality of your service, you might consider bringing it under your ISO 9000 system. The same applies for any other department you consider important. All you have to do is describe its work in written procedures, and ensure that the department does what it says it will do.

The assessor will be happy to check all the departments you include in your manual: the more you include, the more the assessor will charge. But remember that the more departments you include, the more complex your system will be.

Write in the box below those departments that need greater control. Identify what controls are needed to ensure that they perform better.

Table 5.1 Identifying the right departments

Choosing the ISO 9000 departments	
Departments that need improved control or efficiency	Methods by which this could be established (for example, regular reports)
1.	
2.	
3.	
4.	

WHICH PART OF THE STANDARD SHOULD YOU APPLY FOR?

You have to decide which part of the standard you want to be certified against. It could be ISO 9001 or ISO 9002 (BS 5750 Part 1 or Part 2).

ISO 9002 is the basic Standard. It covers your production processes. ISO 9001 is more extensive. As well as production, it includes design.

The important question is, do you design products for your customers? Here are three examples of companies who would want to go for ISO 9001. It is followed by a look at two companies who would want ISO 9002.

1. **You are a jobbing engineering company.** A car manufacturer approaches you with a sketch of a production line for a new car. It wants to be able to tilt the cars on the line, but leaves you to suggest how that would be done. You give the client an estimate, based on the amount of time you reckon your designers will need.

2. **You are a food manufacturer.** A supermarket chain asks you to produce apple pies. The supermarket has no firm idea what the apple pies should contain. In cases like this you usually ask your home economist and your production department to produce some samples for the client to taste.

3. **You install computer networks.** Each client has different equipment, and has different priorities. Because of this, you include in the price the cost of a survey to establish how the client's computer system will be linked. One of your engineers will be assigned to drawing up a set of plans.

The examples quoted above don't involve design as you might imagine it – an artist labouring with pen and paper to produce attractive pictures. Instead you have engineers and other staff whose expertise the client needs to produce solutions.

Here are three cases where you would require ISO 9002.

1. **You are a geological survey company**. An oil company client wants you to do a survey of a new part of the sea bed. The survey results in a standard map, the sort that all your clients get.

2. **You make a range of shelving units**. These are sold on the High Street under your brand name. You don't make 'specials' for anyone, because experience has taught you that customers aren't willing to pay enough or buy in sufficient quantity.

In the two cases quoted above, your customers get a standardised product. You occasionally produce new designs, but they aren't at the request of your customers. In other words, customers don't rely on you to solve their special problems or come up with tailor made solutions.

Case history: even small organisations need ISO 9001

The environment group in a local authority planning department decided that it needed to seek outside contracts, advising other authorities on environmental matters.

The first step the eleven-strong group took was to seek registration to ISO 9000. It knew that many local government organisations require the Standard from its suppliers.

The group provides advice on planning issues. It also provides designs for highways and housing departments. Because design is an important function for the group, it decided to go for ISO 9001.

Table 5.2 (see next page) shows the main clauses. Following the 1994 changes, there is only one difference between ISO 9001 and ISO 9002: Clausee 4.4 (Design control) does not apply to ISO 9002.

Making a choice

Look at it from your customer's point of view. And then consider the potential for internal efficiencies.

What benefits will you get from the extra effort of registering to ISO 9001 (BS 5750 Part 1)?

Your customers: If customers rely on your design skills, registering to ISO 9001 will encourage them to place more of their work with you. If you don't offer design to your customers, there is less value.

Table 5.2 The clauses of ISO 9000

The clauses of the Standard	
Topic	**Clause number**
Management responsibility	4.1 b
Quality system	4.2
Contract review	4.3
Design control	4.4 a
Document and data control	4.5
Purchasing	4.6
Customer-supplied equipment	4.7
Product identification and traceability	4.8
Process control	4.9
Inspection and testing	4.10
Inspection, measuring and test equipment	4.11
Inspection and test status	4.12
Control of non-conforming product	4.13
Corrective and preventative action	4.14
Handling, storage, packaging, preservation and delivery	4.15
Quality records	4.16
Internal quality audits	4.17
Training	4.18
Servicing	4.19
Statistical techniques	4.20

Note: (a) Not in ISO 9002

Internal efficiency: If you want to improve the quality of your design department, consider submitting it to the rigours of ISO 9000, even if it never deals with your customers. ISO 9000 might help you ensure that the designs are more readily accepted by the customer or the production department, and that the designs achieve greater success in the market place.

Case history: Why upgrade to the higher standard?

'We upgraded to ISO 9001 to improve our performance,' said Peter Gavin, Quality Manager of Siemens Lighting, a company which had had ISO 9002 for several years.

'With our design department not previously involved with ISO 9000, the process was a little fragmented,' he said. 'Now the department is fully involved in Contract Review exercises, checking what the customer wants. It means we're offering our customers a better service, especially when they want something quickly.'

'Generally, customers don't know the difference between ISO 9001 and ISO 9002,' he said. 'As long as you have an ISO 9000 certificate, they're happy. Upgrading to ISO 9001 was simply aimed at making us a more effective business.'

One solution is to start by opting for the simpler ISO 9002 (BS 5750 Part 2). Once you have secured registration, you can spend time helping your design department prepare for registration.

Design departments are often quite straightforward places with simple processes operating in a controlled environment. So you should not be put off ISO 9001 unnecessarily. There can be major benefits in including the design department inside the quality system, as the case history above shows.

Table 5.3 Deciding whether to go for the tougher Standard

ISO 9001: FOR AND AGAINST	
For ISO 9001	**Against ISO 9001**
Gives you more control over your business	Makes your system more complex
Gives you greater credibility among your customers	Design may not be an important part of your business
Will improve the effectiveness of your designs	

Starting small

Many companies adopt a gradual approach. They certify their core business, often using a small part of their organisation as a test. They then apply this knowledge to more important and substantial parts of the business.

Case history: How to take it one step at a time

Oasters is a major egg producer, which is vertically integrated. It owns farms that produce cereals, and a mill that turns the cereal into feed for its hens. Oasters also has hatcheries, which rear chicks that become hens. It also has processing plants, which supply liquid egg to caterers for making scrambled egg, and pickled eggs.

The company started by certifying its core businesses: the egg packing station, boiling plant and processing plant.

A year later it got its transport department and its hatchery certified. It expects to certify its farms later, proving that ISO 9000 can be applied to any type of business. It is no coincidence that many top supermarkets buy their eggs from Oasters – and then put the supermarket name on them.

Each new phase becomes successively easier. There is a phrase: 'By the inch it's a cinch'. This might be a useful maxim for companies adopting ISO 9000.

ADVANTAGES OF DOING IT YOURSELF

Some companies prefer to do it themselves, when it comes to installing a quality system, rather than using a consultancy. There are many advantages in this approach.

- You get to know the system inside out. Because you built it, you know how it works. That makes altering it easier.
- Your staff are likely to have been more involved. This means that they will have assumed ownership of the system. There will be less chance that the workforce will reject the system.
- The visible costs are lower than using a consultancy.

READY-MADE MANUALS

You can buy a ready-made manual, often quite cheaply. But there are drawbacks to this approach. Each industry and company is different. So a standard manual can't reflect your special operating methods.

You design a quality system by examining your company's processes, and then writing down those processes as procedures. No ready-made manual can know how your business works.

Also, your staff have to understand why you are asking them to follow certain procedures. An 'imposed' system in which they have no share is unlikely to work.

But some parts of ISO 9000 are common to all businesses. Document control works in the same way in many organisations. Some quality policies are nearly identical.

Most consultants will privately admit they have standard manuals that they adapt for each client.

So if you feel this would set you off in the right direction, use a ready-made manual. But remember that just because you can point to a finished manual does not mean that you have a quality system in place. The assessor will want to see evidence that your staff actually use the system. And the real benefits of ISO 9000 come from having a workforce that believes in quality assurance. Having a manual does not in itself give you any advantage.

USING A CONSULTANCY

Many companies seek the help of a management consultancy to help them implement ISO 9000. The advantages of using a consultancy are as follows.

■ You don't have to re-invent the wheel. The consultancy knows how a quality system works, and knows the pitfalls. It will save you hours agonizing over the best way to design a corrective action procedure. This leads to the second advantage.

■ You install the system faster. These days companies are much leaner than they were. Where there were once departments full of people who could be released for six months, now one individual often has to do several jobs at once. In these cases, companies sometimes have to put their plans for certification on hold because, six months after starting the ISO 9000 project, they find it is taking more time than they imagined.

A consultancy will help you design a quality system for your business. It will identify what procedures you need. It will teach your staff how to write procedures and how to do audits. If you use a consultancy, you may rely greatly on it at the beginning, and gradually have less involvement as your expertise and the system develops.

The consultancy's last task will be to return to do a pre-assessment visit. This is an audit identical to the one the certification body will carry out. It checks that your system is running well and that it will gain the certification body's approval.

CONSULTANCY PROBLEMS

It is important to assess the consultancy's style and experience before appointing it. This will prevent you suffering the problems that are common to companies who use consultants.

One of my colleagues was talking to a Local Authority about its newly installed quality system. In the manual he found references to 'The quality of the double glazing'. The original consultants seem to have based the manual on a previous job, which had been for a window manufacturer.

This means that the consultancy will have introduced procedures which were suitable for a double glazing company. The local authority will have had to alter its systems to meet the new procedures, rather than the other way around. It will have meant reduced efficiency, extra costs, and a poorer service for local people.

Failure to understand the industry is a common complaint. A packaging company said, 'The consultants didn't understand our business. After they left, we spent ages changing the procedures so that they matched our needs. If we were to use another consultancy, we'd want to make sure they knew more about packaging'.

One building company used a consultant who was an engineer by trade. Soon the company found that its consultant had a different attitude to quality. Used to working to very small tolerances, he was asking the company to adopt standards of accuracy that the company would have difficulty maintaining. Because of the variations in the materials they use, builders accept tolerances that would be unthinkable in other industries. Eventually, the company got rid of the consultant, but not before valuable time had been wasted.

If you use a consultancy, make sure your staff are involved. Otherwise, they will end up with an 'imposed system'. It can cause the system to break down, because staff won't be interested in doing jobs or keeping records the way the system says they should.

HOW TO ASSESS A CONSULTANCY

The lessons from this are straightforward. Don't use a consultancy if it can't give you the names of other companies in your industry whom it has helped.

Before appointing the consultancy, check with those clients to assess their satisfaction with the work.

Don't measure consultancies mainly on cost. The cost to your business of installing the wrong sort of system will be enormous; and the difference between the right consultants and the wrong ones will, in terms of their fees, be small in comparison.

Ensure, too, that the consultancy doesn't want to simply install a complete 'turnkey' system. A good consultancy will oblige your staff to do much of the work, because that is the only way they will take 'ownership' of the system.

Make sure you meet in advance the actual consultant who is to do the work for you. He may be different from the sales person you initially met. Check that you can get on with the consultant before signing a contract.

Make sure you pay according to time spent. Never write a cheque in advance for the whole amount.

Action List: checking a consultancy

- How many quality consultants does it have?

- What experience does it have of your industry? (don't be a guinea pig)

- Can it give you the names of recent clients who have been registered successfully?

- What does it charge per day? Are there any other costs or expenses? Go for value and experience. Accepting the cheapest quote may cost you dear in the long run.

- What timescale does it anticipate? How much time will it need to get you registered to ISO 9000? In other words, what would the total cost be?

- How far is it located from you? (The further the distance, the less chance of good service.)

- How efficient and knowledgeable does it seem to be?

- Does it seem to understand your needs?

- Does it understand your process or work flow?

- How high are its standards? (Standards that are too high or too detailed could cripple your business).

■ Will it give you a firm quotation of costs, together with a list of what it plans to achieve, and with dates? This will let you check progress.

■ Is the consultancy certified to ISO 9000?

■ Which consultant will be assigned to you? What is your impression of him?

■ Is he a Registered Lead Assessor?

■ Does the consultant know the minimum system that is acceptable to the certification body? (thus avoiding unnecessarily large systems)?

Don't take the first consultant who knocks on your door. Ask two or three consultancies to offer proposals, and evaluate them using the action list below.

SUMMARY

■ You should apply for ISO 9001 (BS 5750 Part 1) if your customers ask you to design products or services for them.

■ If you don't carry out design, or your design department is purely for internal purposes, you should go for ISO 9002 (BS 5750 Part 2).

■ Going for the more advanced standard could give your business a competitive advantage.

■ You may find it better to start small, by initially certifying just your main processes or one division. You can add your design department or other parts of the business later.

■ You can implement ISO 9000 yourself, or get a consultancy to help you. There are advantages and disadvantages to both these strategies. The same applies to buying ready-made manuals.

6

THE SECRETS OF ISO 9000

◆

In this chapter you'll discover:

- ■ The seven principles of ISO 9000.
- ■ How to set up a manual.
- ■ How to write procedures.

CRACKING THE CODE

Every religion has its rituals and codes. Computer experts talk in techno-babble that baffles ordinary PC users.

So it is with ISO 9000 (BS 5750). It is written in a special language. It uses certain words that are pregnant with meaning, and quite mysterious to the uninitiated.

You have to understand the words and the ideas that lie behind them before you can implement the system. The principles of ISO 9000 are very simple. It's just that the clauses are phrased in a complex and abstract way.

The clauses incorporate every possible eventuality, like lawyers do. This makes the sentences long and difficult to understand.

Your task is to convert the generalisations of ISO 9000 into a specific system that reflects the needs of your organisation.

Appendix 2 contains a glossary of the terms used in ISO 9000. Here we focus on the main concepts of the standard, and explore their meaning.

THE SEVEN PRINCIPLES OF ISO 9000

ISO 9000 is founded on seven principles of quality management. They are as follows.

1. **Get organised** – ISO 9000 expects you to have an organisation chart. It expects people to have defined roles. If everyone knows what they are responsible for, there is more chance that things will get done.

2. **Have written procedures** – This means writing down the way your main processes work. Take a simple example: imagine you make small pumps. Each pump contains a number of components. The components have to be installed in the right order. So it is important to write down

exactly how the pump should be assembled. This is the assembly procedure. Procedures have to be written down. Later in this chapter we look at how to write procedures.

3. **Control key documents** – In the previous paragraph, we looked at a procedure for assembling a pump. But what happens when you introduce a new, improved pump? You'll need to issue a new procedure. This new procedure will tell staff how to assemble the new pump.

At this point there is a danger. You now have two procedures, the new one and the old one. If people continue to assemble the new motor in the old way, the product won't work.

So it is important to issue the new document formally and recall the old one.

The documents that you issue in this way are called *controlled documents*. To keep track of them, you have to know how many you have issued, and to whom they have gone. That makes the process of updating them much easier.

4. **Keep records** – Good records allow you to trace what happened when something went wrong. They also allow you to prove that procedures were followed.

In one assessment, the auditor spotted a works order containing the words 'Colour to be confirmed'. He asked the production staff what had happened. 'We rang up the customer, and they confirmed they wanted Cobalt Blue. We produced it, and they were happy', said the manager. 'But you didn't document the colour', said the assessor, and duly faulted the company.

5. **Carry out regular checks** – ISO 9000 expects you to check or test your product. This applies to service companies just as much as manufacturing businesses. These can be checks during the production process (to make sure that the product is right). Or they can be audits to make sure the system is working (for example, checking that people are following procedures).

We examine in Chapter 8 exactly what kinds of checks you should do.

6. **Identify faults and correct them** – In ISO 9000 'corrective action' follows when you have identified a problem. The product might not perform as it is supposed to. It might not be stored the way the procedure says it should. Or perhaps a service was delivered 24 hours later than you said it would be.

When you have identified a fault, you need to make sure it doesn't happen again. Some corrective actions will be obvious and quick, such as when you find an operator failing to keep records. Other problems may be more difficult, such as understanding why a product keeps breaking down.

7. **Communicate well** – ISO 9000 tries to prevent error by improving communications. That means communication between departments and within departments. It means ensuring that everyone knows what their job is.

Case history: the anonymous company

One company admitted that, before it introduced ISO 9000, 25 per cent of its output was 'outside the customer's specification'. One in every four items it made was wrong.

A Hertfordshire-based business with a £40 million turnover, the company makes components for industrial users.

It was so ashamed of its history that it refused to let its name be mentioned in this book. 'It would make us look fools,' said the Managing Director.

Back in 1990, scrap and re-work was costing the company £26,000 a month. Now the cost is only £1,500. The savings were achieved by ISO 9000.

It's as though the company is getting a cheque for £24,500 every month, for ever. It can spend it in any way it wants. It can add it to its profits, spend it on new plant, or give everyone a pay rise.

Losing profit through poor quality is a surprisingly expensive business. Most companies don't realise how much it really costs them.

Surveys have found companies who are losing 40 per cent of their turnover on 'the cost of quality'. Yet companies rarely count all their losses, because many of them are hidden.

SETTING UP A MANUAL

For many people, manuals are a symbol of what is worst about ISO 9000. They represent a bureaucratic dead weight. Many managers say they have never opened their manuals. This statement tells you a lot. It tells you that the manager was not involved in writing his part of the manual. If he hasn't read it, he can't know what the quality system requires of him.

But the manual has positive benefits. It is the home of your system. It is where people look if they aren't sure about something. It is where all the procedures and documentation is kept. Normally, it is easily identifiable, being in a special colour or having a special cover and spine.

Tip

A computer or word processor-based system will make life easier for you. Many companies now have a computer-based manual.

When you revise a document, the computer tells you who to send copies to, and prints out a revised master list. Much of this work is repetitive and systematic, and that is what computers enjoy.

Remember that managers will still need a paper-based copy of the manual.

Three manuals

With their quality policy at the top of the pyramid, companies sometimes have three manuals (or three levels of manual), reflecting three levels of detail. These are:

- System manual.
- Procedures manual.
- Work instructions manual.

Each department will have its own procedures and work instructions, as Figure 6.1 shows.

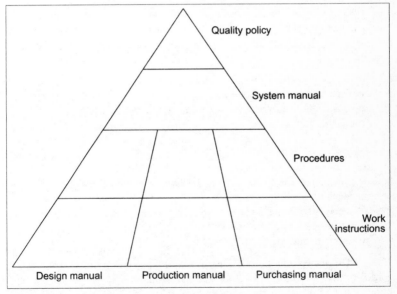

Figure 6.1 The quality pyramid

The system should flow vertically – from general policy statements in the system manual to detailed step-by-step actions in the work instructions.

The system should also flow horizontally. For example, there should be audits for each department.

The manuals are usually ring binders. Inside the binder, the procedures are inserted into transparent sleeves to protect them from wear and doodlers. Other companies bind the procedures into a book. That way the procedures can't get separated; but updating one procedure means reprinting the whole document.

As with all parts of ISO 9000, you should design the manual to meet your needs. It's up to you to decide how many tiers to have, and what to include. Not every company has three tiers. The transport department of a health board has a total of 68 pages in one single manual.

The names given to the manuals and their contents vary. For example, a system manual is often called a policy manual. Procedures are sometimes called work instructions. You can call them whatever you want, but the system of tiers generally works well.

You should make it easy for people to use the manuals, by having tables of contents and cross-references to other manuals.

The System manual

The system manual is at a strategic level, and is sometimes used as a marketing document by being given to customers. It states the company's approach to quality, and covers the clause on Organization (4.1.2). It often includes:

- The quality policy (discussed in Chapter 4).
- Information on the company's quality structure (normally presented as an organisation chart). This is discussed further in Chapter 9.
- Information on responsibilities, identifying who is responsible for managing quality. This is normally presented as outline job descriptions for departmental managers and the quality manager. This, too, is discussed further in Chapter 9.
- An outline of the main procedures, which explain how the company manages its quality system.
- You may also include marketing information about the business. This might include a description of the products you make, the equipment you possess and your skills or certificates.

The system manual should not contain too much detail. The place for detail is in the procedures or work instructions manual. Any details that change frequently should go in these lower level manuals. This will save regular changes having to be made to the system manual.

The Procedures manual

The procedures manual is usually at a departmental level, and is confidential to the company. It tells the reader how quality is controlled in each department, and what checks are carried out.

FRIDAYS (CRANBROOK) LIMITED

QUALITY PROCEDURE   Q.P. 4.5

ISSUE: 3
APPROVED: C. Clearer
DATE: 6.08.92
PAGE: 1 OF 2

TITLE   CONTROL OF PROCESS METHOD INSTRUCTION SHEETS

OBJECTIVE   To control the generation (where applicable) issue and amendement of instruction sheets for production methods and machine operating manuals.

ITEM: PROCEDURE

1   PRODUCTION MANAGER

In conjunction with the Quality Manager an Instruction sheet or machine operating manual is prepared for each separate process and machine to include:-

NUMBER
DATE OF ISSUE
NAME OF PROCESS OR MACHINE
SPECIAL INSTRUCTIONS
MATERIAL TO USE
EQUIPMENT TO USE
TECHNIQUE OF OPERATION
INSPECTION AND TEST METHODS (Q.P. 4.6)
AUTHORISATION IS BY SIGNING

2   DEPARTMENTAL HEAD

All instruction sheets are authorised by signing and copies are issued to appropriate staff and display locations. Each display location is the responsiblity of a nominated member of staff. A register is kept of all holders and nominated persons responsible for display locations.

3   PRODUCTION MANAGER

Amended Instruction sheets and machine operating manuals are issued to all holders. One copy of the superseded sheets or manuals is marked superseded and filed. The register is amended accordingly.

4   HOLDERS

Copies of previous Instruction sheets and manuals are destroyed.

5   PRODUCTION STAFF

Process and machine operation are carried out in accordance with the relevant up to date Instruction sheets and machine manual.

Figure 6.2 Specimen procedure

The procedures should be laid out in a way that reflects your company's processes. The manual should not slavishly follow the Standard from clause 4.1 to 4.20.

The manual should show how the company conforms to each clause of the Standard. That means including procedures to cover all applicable clauses of the Standard. But you don't have to conform to clauses in the Standard that don't relate to your business. For example, if you don't carry out servicing, you don't need to refer to it.

When Fridays develops a new product (see Figure 6.2), it produces a tailor-made instruction sheet. This tells the operator what material to use, what techniques are involved, and what inspection methods are required. This ensures that the company's products are planned, and manufactured to a consistent standard.

The Work Instructions manual

The work instructions describe in detail how specific tasks are performed. The work instructions (which are sometimes called local instructions) often include drawings or pictures, and may indicate standards of workmanship. They may include specifications provided by the customer.

Some companies decide not to have work instructions, because the nature of the work does not require this level of detail.

To decide what to include, ask yourself, 'What would I need to tell a new employee, so that he can do the job properly?' You don't need to tell a secretary how to type; but you may need a work instruction showing how letters should be laid out.

Tip

If you are looking to keep your manual light, try having just two manuals.

- The first manual will describe the system. Here you confirm that you carry out audits, or carry out design control.
- The second manual contains the procedures. These explain how audits are carried out or what training records are kept.

Case history: The Blood Transfusion Service

Work instructions can help all kinds of organisations. At a Blood Transfusion Service centre, a nurse revealed that there is more than one way to take blood.

'I was trained to take blood in Birmingham,' she said. 'Then I went to work in Coventry. There the nurses told me, "That's not how we do it". They insisted that we re-learn a different method.'

Blood donors are fond of their blood. They like to think it is being well looked after. The thought of confused nurses and wasted blood is enough to make them demand it back.

Part of the Blood Transfusion Service is now certified to ISO 9000. It means that new nurses can learn the procedures quickly. Nurses who move to another area won't have to learn a different technique. And there is less chance of errors occurring.

A fourth manual: forms and records

You will need to control records and forms formally, so many firms keep them in a fourth manual. The manual will hold:

■ Records which the system requires to keep, such as records of inspection.
■ Forms used for audits or purchasing.
■ Other documents, such as codes of practice, international standards, or regulations.

Avoid a large manual

A large manual will hang around your business like a millstone. Only include in it those activities that are absolutely essential to your business. Don't write procedures for processes that don't affect quality. If you write them into your manual, the assessor will insist on checking that you comply absolutely with the terms of your manual.

Case history: The manual that kept growing

Outset is a charity that provides computer training for disabled people, thus equipping them for employment. It decided to get ISO 9000 to satisfy its corporate funders and to improve its quality.

Outset decided to include its PR manager within its quality system, because fund raising is an essential process for a charity.

The PR manager decided to have a checklist for organising her events. Then she thought of having a checklist to evaluate the success of the event. Soon she had a checklist to check her checklists.

It was clearly getting out of hand; and with the help of severe pruning the PR department has now reduced its procedures to a sensible number.

WRITING PROCEDURES

You must involve your staff in writing procedures or work instructions. The right people for this task are the managers and staff who manage and run the departments that need procedures.

The Quality Manager is the wrong person to do the job. If he writes the procedures, the quality system will never be taken to heart by the workforce.

Staff need to be shown how to write procedures. This is one area in which staff feel most vulnerable. You can demonstrate how to write procedures in a formal training session. You should take a typical work activity, and show staff how to convert it into a procedure.

Procedures should be written in a standard format. This will make it easy for staff to understand a procedure if they move departments. It will also help people see how work flows from one department to the next.

You will need to number all the procedures, so that they can be stored in the manual in sequence. It also helps everyone to know precisely which procedure is under discussion at any time. A typical number would be 'ST 005 Handling', meaning the fifth procedure for the stores department, which covers the handling of goods.

Don't make procedures too complicated. The average reading age is only nine years. In Britain, this is the reading level of the Sun newspaper. That is why it sells four million copies every day. It follows that complex procedures will be ignored, because no one will understand them. So bear in mind the following tips:

- Write in the active tense ('Operators should protect the product'), rather than the passive voice ('The product should be protected by the operators').
- Use simple short words. Avoid long abstract words like implementation, amalgamation or consideration.
- Use verbs to express the meaning. Say, 'Alter the document', not 'The alteration of the document'.
- Use short sentences. If your sentence is over 25 words, few staff will understand it. Break up a long sentence into two smaller sentences.

- Don't have unnecessary sections in each procedure. Many quality procedures are prefaced with sections defining the scope, definitions or references. Sometimes the actual procedure doesn't start until after two or three pages of quality-babble. Ask yourself, will anyone wade through all this verbiage?
- Avoid meaningless procedures.
- Avoid using absolute words like 'always' or 'never'. These will come back to haunt you. The assessor will be watching for these words. If your manual says you *always* contact your customers to check their orders, he will ask for evidence that you do it for every job. Inevitably, he will find a few occasions when you have failed to do it, and will mark this as a non-conformance. It is much simpler to use the words 'wherever possible' or 'normally'.

We look at procedures again in Chapter 10, where we consider what to include and what to reject.

SUMMARY

- The principles of ISO 9000 require you to have written procedures, to control the issue of key documents, to keep records and make regular checks on the system.
- It also requires you to identify faults and correct them, and to communicate well.
- It is quite common for a company to lose 25 per cent of its revenue through quality failings.
- ISO 9000 is usually collated into two or three tiered manuals.
- The top tier manual describes briefly how the company conforms to ISO 9000. The second tier contain detailed procedures for staff to follow.
- Procedures should be brief, simple and direct. You should avoid words like 'always'.

7

IMPROVE YOUR PURCHASING AND DESIGN

◆

In this chapter, you'll learn about:

■ The hidden structure of ISO 9000.
■ Improving the quality of your suppliers.
■ Getting your designs right first time.

THE HIDDEN STRUCTURE OF ISO 9000

ISO 9000 (BS 5750) is structured in a way that makes little sense. The clauses hop from one topic to another with a cheerful disregard for logic.

You can group the clauses into four areas. They are: your work, your people, your system and your information. They are shown in Table 7.1 below.

Table 7.1 A summary of the Standard

Your work
Nine clauses in ISO 9000 govern the work you do. In this book, the Work clauses have been laid out in the way that your product or service moves through the business. The Work clauses start when you receive an order or a request to tender, and finish at the moment you deliver the finished product.

Your people	Your system	Your information
Two clauses relate to your staff. The clauses ask you to manage staff in such a way that everyone knows what is going on.	Four clauses cover the quality system. They make sure you carry out audits and control key documents, so that your business will run smoothly.	Three clauses make sure that your decisions are based on solid information. They ask you to identify your products and to keep records.

Table 7.1 does not list the clauses in the same order as the Standard. As we saw at the beginning of this chapter, ISO 9000 numbers the clauses in an

apparently random way. The arrangement in *this* book aims to show the underlying structure of the standard.

Each of the clauses is listed in Figure 7.1 below. This shows the same information as Table 7.1, but in more detail.

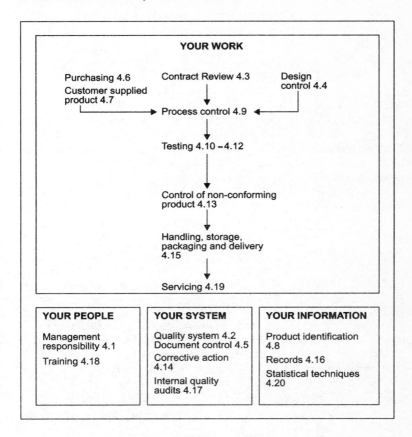

Figure 7.1 The real structure of ISO 9000

Next we look at each of the four groups (and the clauses in them) in more detail.

Your work

The clauses that relate to your work are shown in the big box in Figure 7.1. As you might expect, there are more clauses about how to manage your processes than anything else.

In the chart, the clauses are in the order in which your work flows through the business. We start with purchasing because it's straightforward.

The *purchasing* clauses ask you to make sure that you buy systematically, and that you assess the quality of your suppliers. There is no point in having a top quality production line if you are let down by your raw materials.

Then we look at *design*. ISO 9001 wants you to make sure you organise the design department properly, and that you give it briefs which contain all the necessary information. The Standard also asks you to check that the design department gives you what you asked for.

If you intend to go for ISO 9002 (BS 5750 Part 2), you can ignore the section on design.

Then we look at what happens when you receive an order. This is called *contract review*. It is designed to prevent you from rushing blindly into production without thinking how you will do it.

The *process control* clauses ask you to manage your production process by writing down how it will be carried out. You also need to monitor your process, to make sure it remains at the right quality.

The monitoring of your process is expanded upon in the next clauses, which ask you to check your process regularly. The Standard calls this *Inspection and testing*.

If you produce any sub-standard goods, you have to decide what to do with them. This is called *Control of non-conforming product*.

The Standard also asks you to watch the way your product is handled. It covers this under *Handling, storage, packaging, preservation and delivery*.

Once you have delivered your product, you may have to provide *servicing*. There is a clause for this activity).

Now that you have seen the structure of the Work clauses, it is time to look at them one by one. In later chapters, we'll look at the clauses relating to your people, system and your information.

IMPROVING THE QUALITY OF YOUR SUPPLIERS

Every business buys goods and services. Some of the biggest purchasers are found in local authorities, schools and other non-profit organisations.

Do you know how much of your revenue goes to your suppliers? It's worth finding out, because in some organisations, raw materials account for 50 per cent of the costs.

If your suppliers are averagely inefficient, you're paying for their mistakes. You're paying for faulty components, for down-time while a problem is fixed, or for the time you spend asking for a credit note. Your customers are paying for those errors. And those same customers may decide to find another supplier whose costs do not include such faults.

If you can cut the proportion of faulty deliveries, you will save your organisation a lot of money.

There are only two ways to do this. Either your existing suppliers reduce their quality problems, or else you find new suppliers. In the car industry, suppliers responsible for halting a production line are charged by the minute. And the cost of stopping a giant car plant are astronomical.

You probably don't have the purchasing power of a car manufacturer, so you may have to find a less dramatic way of controlling your suppliers.

ISO 9000 wants you to assess your suppliers (or sub-contractors, as it calls them). If a supplier has satisfactorily delivered all your catering needs for the last two years, that's all that the standard needs to know. If a supplier is certified to ISO 9000, you might take this as adequate evidence of the company's quality.

Producing an approved suppliers list is a valuable exercise because it saves you time whenever you want to buy a standard item.

Here ISO 9000 is also in step with current management thinking. 'Partnership sourcing' is a vogue word for getting close to your suppliers and treating them as colleagues not enemies. Buying the cheapest possible goods at the lowest possible price is not a suitable strategy for the 21st century. It will inevitably bring problems of poor quality goods, unreliable deliveries and lack of consistency. Japanese companies have pointed the way in reducing the number of suppliers they deal with, and developing a long term relationship with them.

You can ask your suppliers to get ISO 9000. Or you can ask them to apply the same quality principles that you do.

Keeping an eye on your suppliers

The ISO 9000 assessor will ask you how you monitor the quality of your suppliers' goods. You can do this either at goods inward inspection (which we discuss later), or when you use their product. You should also consider conducting audits of key suppliers at their premises to ensure that they match your standards.

When you find their product or service defective, don't simply fix it or return it. Ask the supplier to tell you what corrective action it plans to take.

Completing the purchase order properly

The Standard expects you to order goods on a proper purchase order. Big organisations do that as a matter of course, but smaller ones often order goods over the telephone.

Some purchasing managers and office managers are driven wild by goods turning up addressed to secretaries, and for which there is no paperwork. How can you keep a check on what you're buying if you have no records?

ISO 9000 doesn't stop you phoning an order to a supplier, but the order should be confirmed in writing.

You can use the purchase order to improve the supplier's quality, by requiring the supplier to undertake specific tests or keep certain records.

Write in the box below the main things you buy, and what you must do to get better quality and prevent errors.

Table 7.2 Improving our purchasing

BETTER PURCHASING CONTROL		
The important things we buy	The quality faults we find	What we must do to ensure we get the right quality?

Companies who supply you with a service

Don't forget to include the companies who supply services, if they affect the quality of what you do. A manufacturer might need to check its haulage company, its laboratory analysis supplier, or even its certification body.

If you are a service organisation, you will want to get the best supplier to service your photocopiers, courier your documents, and print your stationery.

Managing your contractors

Contractors are a particularly important group. Customers often judge you by the work your sub-contractors do. Often they assume that the sub-contractor's staff are your own. Take a building site where new houses are being built, and which is festooned with flags and signs promoting the builder's name. All the bricklayers, carpenters and plumbers belong to a sub-contractor, and the quality of their work directly affects the builder's image. Inadequate controls on the sub-contractor can subsequently lead to leaking drains, collapsing kitchen units, and cracks in the walls.

An important part of supplier assessment is judging a supplier's on-going performance. You need good communication between purchasing and production, so that faulty deliveries are duly noted and changes made if required.

Changing the order

Orders or specifications are sometimes changed as a project progresses. You should state in writing how these changes will be made.

LOOKING AFTER OTHER PEOPLE'S GOODS

ISO 9000 wants you to take care of any goods entrusted to you by your customers. Here ISO 9000 reveals its engineering origins.

Imagine you're an engineering works which is making a modern windmill. Your skill lies in welding the metal so that the windmill stays upright. But there will be specialist bits that you won't try to make. They include computer chips for changing the angle of the blades, and the batteries for storing energy.

Your customer may decide to buy these parts, and send them to you. ISO 9000 calls them 'Customer-supplied product'; others call them 'Free issue' goods.

You have to look after them to make sure they don't come to harm. And you have to ensure they don't get put into another customer's product.

Here are some more examples of Customer-supplied product:

- A roadside assistance company like the AA receives its customers' broken-down cars. So do garages.
- A laboratory receives samples from customers for analysis.
- A veterinary surgery has customers' pets on its premises.
- A direct mail house has stationery belonging to its customers.

■   A laundry has its customers' clothes. A hotel may have its guests'
    valuables, or be given their shoes for cleaning.

If you receive goods that belong to your customers, you might like to
consider how they are protected, and whether you could improve the system.

GETTING YOUR DESIGNS RIGHT FIRST TIME

In chapter 5 we discussed whether you want to include design in your
quality system. If you have decided to exclude design, by choosing ISO
9002, you can ignore this section and go to the chapter summary. If you've
opted for ISO 9001, read on.

   Manufacturing companies are accustomed to designing new products. But
service organisations don't always recognise that they are producing designs,
partly because they are often produced in an informal way. Designs in
service organisations include:

Insurance	a new insurance policy
Retailer	a new look for a store
Hospital	a new surgical operation
School	a new timetable

In service companies the design work is often done by operations staff,
rather than a design department. In an IT consultancy, the consultant may
carry out a survey of a client's problem, and then design a solution. To give
the client proper service, this design work needs to be properly reviewed.

Case history: Designs behind closed doors

The UK's top vinyl floorcovering company launches new
designs twice a year, in the Spring and Autumn. The design
department is staffed with creative and talented people who
operate in almost complete isolation from the rest of the business.

Twice a year, the department throws open its doors and displays
its new marvels. One or two of its designs will be top sellers,
many sell reasonably well, and a couple will fail.

The marketing department pleads to be allowed to test the designs for consumer approval prior to launch. But the Design director is firmly against it. 'Asking 50 housewives in a wet hall in Wigan what they think about design tells you nothing,' he says.

In the end, Design gets its own way, because the company is worried that the Design Director might resign.

The problems are clear for all to see. There is no communication, no design briefs, no checking to see whether the designs meet the market's requirements. Yet applying common sense rules of ISO 9000 could reduce confusion, eliminate waste and improve sales.

Establishing best practice in design

Good practice in design includes:

- Producing a programme of work (so that everyone knows what the department is working to achieve). This would be broken down into key events and deadlines.
- Writing procedures for the department's processes and drawings and specification (so that staff know what is expected of them, drawings don't get lost, and work is produced on time).
- Making sure that design staff are properly managed, trained and equipped.
- Identifying the people in other departments with whom design needs to liaise. This includes marketing and production. Asking, 'Do our customers want the design, and can our production department produce it?' is the basis of the design brief.
- Knowing what the law requires (including health, safety and the environment).
- Making sure the product meets the needs of the market (whether in terms of attractiveness, function, performance, reliability or cost). This is done by having proper design briefs and by checking that the design meets the brief.
- Holding design review meetings to ensure that new designs are developed as smoothly as possible.
- Ensuring that design changes are made in a structured way.

Asked to explain how the luxury car maker Jaguar had jumped from the bottom of the US reliability ratings to near the top, a top Jaguar engineer said, 'We started putting figures to things. We started being systematic. We started taking decisions based on facts. Before, we'd try something, and if it didn't work, we'd try something different.'

It was no coincidence that Jaguar was installing ISO 9000 when the company's reliability made its giant leap forward. And just as logically, US car buyers started buying Jaguars in large numbers again.

Put in the box below the types of design you undertake. Remember that design is involved where you least expect it. If you launch a new service or help a customer decide the layout of his laboratory, you are involved with design.

Table 7.3 What designs do we produce?

Design activities	
What designs or development do we undertake?	**How should we control our design process?**

SUMMARY

- ■ ISO 9000 can be divided into four main areas: your work process, your people, your system, and your information.
- ■ You can improve the quality of your suppliers by having detailed purchase orders, by monitoring what they deliver, and by keeping records.
- ■ If you have products that belong to your customers, you have to look after them properly. With ISO 9000, this means having written procedures.
- ■ If you choose ISO 9001 (BS 5750 Part 1), your design department will have to conform to the Standard. This means having procedures to ensure that the designs are produced in a professional manner.
- ■ The design department must be properly structured. Only qualified people should produce designs (whether qualified by education, training or experience). The department should liaise with other departments. Briefs must be comprehensive. You should check that designs meet the brief. Design changes must be noted in writing.

8

MANAGING YOUR WORK

◆

In this chapter, you'll learn about:

- The benefits of checking incoming orders.
- Managing your work process.
- Reducing errors through better inspection.
- Four strategies for when things go wrong.
- Handling and storing your product.
- Enhanced servicing.

CHECKING THE ORDER

We have looked at how ISO 9000 fits together. And we have looked at the purchasing department and the design department. Now we can look at what happens when an order arrives.

The first clause we need to examine is Contract Review (clause 4.3). This covers what happens when you receive an order or a contract. Many companies would call it 'order processing'.

Remember that ISO 9000 originated with the military. It assumes you get large contracts for battleships and laser-guided nuclear weapons. If you are in this line of work, you should check the order carefully to make sure you have all the parts you need (plutonium, large sheets of metal, and so on).

This is a valuable exercise for any business that sends out tenders and receives detailed contracts. After all, the words of the contract may be different from the original tender.

This clause is also useful for organisations that provide a service:

- A client who wants you to insure the contents of his house may have remembered to add some expensive jewellery to the list, which he forgot to mention when he asked for a quote on the telephone.

■ If you have a client who wants you to manage his data processing facilities, it is worth starting the work in a professional manner. Have you got the right staff? Have you got a plan? Have you got the right structure for managing the work? Contract review will encourage you to ask these questions.

■ If you sell lots of small value items, such as a mail order company might do, you might want to check that you have the item in stock. If you haven't, you will need to talk to the customer.

For really small items, Contract Review is not of great value. Assessors will accept that when your staff press the 'enter' button on their cash till, they have verified that the customer has supplied the right money and that the goods are fit for sale.

What happens in your organisation when a contract or order arrives? Does it go straight to production, without any checks? Many companies are so pleased to get business that it does not occur to them to query it. Yet if you fail to fulfil the order properly, the customer may decide never to buy from you again.

Tip

You can hold Contract Review meetings throughout the duration of a project. This will ensure that the project is going as planned.

Avoiding bad debts

There are other advantages in checking an order. One of them is financial control.

In one construction company, new orders are sent to the chief executive, who does a credit check on them before allowing production staff to execute the order. Needless to say, this company often refuses work and rarely has problems getting paid.

One advertising agency went into liquidation because a client went bust owing them a lot of money. The ad agency boss learnt from his mistake and on setting up a new agency insisted on strict credit checking. On one occasion a major car manufacturer offered the agency its account. On finding that he could not get insurance cover for this company, the chief executive turned down the account, even though it would have doubled the size of his agency.

What topics do *you* need to check when an order or a contract arrives? Ask yourself how many things you have on your checklist for when you receive an order or contract.

MANAGING THE WORK

Now it is time to enter the shopfloor, to see what happens when you fulfil an order. This is clause 4.9, called Process Control.

In this clause, ISO 9000 wants you to plan your production. And it wants you to carry out your production in a controlled manner. That means writing down how the work is supposed to be carried out, and then getting everyone to use that method.

ISO 9000 also wants you to state the quality of workmanship you expect (Are your products free from blemishes?)

Describing the method of work

You need to define how your work processes work. This will call for diagrams, showing how designs are made, orders arrive, production planned and executed, and the goods stored and despatched.

Tip

Chapter 4 takes an initial look at this subject in the section called 'Describe how the company's processes work'. Chapter 6 has more information about writing procedures in the section called 'Writing procedures'.

This is a valuable time for analysis. Ask yourself whether you process work in the best way. Are there ways you could do it better? Do staff have to move the product a long distance to the next process? Do they have to stretch? Are there dangers that could be prevented?

Most important of all, do your processes benefit the customer? For example, could you involve the customer more at a prototype stage? Do you insist that customers take fixed amounts or sizes? Could you be more flexible?

Method of work in a service organisation

Service companies have work processes just as much as manufacturers. For example, a bank may have branches which receive cash, enter the details on the computer, and store the cash in a till. If they receive cheques, they would need to check that each is correctly filled out before entering the details on computer. A different process will take place when the customer wants to take money from his account.

Later, the money will need to be transferred to a security firm, and analyses will be done on the day's trading. Staff may need to check customers' records. They may write to customers, offering them more credit or telling them to reduce their overdraft.

All these transactions need to be documented, so that staff know what is required of them. Standardising the procedures will help to prevent mistakes, and provide a more consistent service.

In a purely service business, such as consultancy, the processes may involve:

■ Commissioning (including selling the job, and agreeing the method of work).
■ Execution (which might include analysis).
■ Completion (which may involve reporting or implementation).

A nursing home would need to write procedures for:

■ Nursing care (such as staffing levels, the use of care plans and nursing treatments).
■ Dietary care (including menu selection and provision of special menus).
■ Administration (such as admission and discharge, and fire procedures).

A solicitor's practice will need procedures for taking instructions from clients, for progressing a case, and for case monitoring.

Checklists

Service companies sometimes use checklists to keep a check on the progress of a job. It helps to ensure that no stages are left out. And it demonstrates to a quality auditor that the process has been properly followed. Typical examples are:

■ A solicitor involved with house conveyancing.
■ An accountant undertaking a client's tax return.
■ A public relations consultancy planning an event.

Table 8.1 The flow of work in our organisation.

Work flow in our organisation

In the box above, draw a diagram showing the work that takes place in your organisation. Keep it simple. Just show who uses your product or service, how they order it, and what work takes place in producing it. Show, too, how your product gets to the customer.

Processes which can't be checked

Parachutes, air bags and ring-pull cans are three examples of process that can't be checked except in use. ISO 9000 calls them 'special processes'. You only find out if they work when the customer operates them. And if they fail, there can sometimes be terrible consequences.

To overcome this disadvantage, you need to take special care in making these products. Constant checking is the normal solution. It applies to services as well:

- There is only one way of telling if a steak is cooked all the way through, and that is to eat it. (With today's microwave and cook–chill catering methods, there are more chances of error than before).
- When the surgeon sews up a patient after an operation, how does he know he hasn't left a pair of scissors inside the patient's body? It happens.
- How does an architect know that a building is going to stay upright – until after it is built?

You might consider if any of your products are hidden from view once completed. Are any of your processes uncheckable? Are you confident that nothing can go wrong?

REDUCING ERRORS THROUGH BETTER INSPECTION

No one is perfect, and mistakes take place in the best run places. That is why you need to carry out regular checks on the work.

Your procedures will need to state *who* is responsible for testing, and *what* tests should be made.

You need to keep records of what is inspected. If a customer finds glass in your product and takes you to court, your records could prove 'due diligence'. In other words, they could demonstrate that you honestly sought to prevent this sort of mishap from occurring.

You should be able to see whether a product has passed or failed a test. Failed products may be identified by being placed in a coloured bin. Or you might have a special area of the factory floor marked with red lines.

The first items to check are your purchases. ISO 9000 calls this 'receiving inspection'. Some companies call it 'goods inwards'. If you don't check your purchases, how do you know whether you get what you ordered? If you order 100 items and receive only 90, you lose a lot of money.

Some service companies are heavy users of raw materials.

- A photographic studio needs the right film stocks.
- An office cleaning company needs the right cleaning materials.
- A computer network company needs the right cables.

If you buy products that don't relate to your quality system (for example, the window cleaner's work), you can omit them from receiving inspection.

If you are confident about the quality of certain goods (for example, from another part of your organisation), you can state that you don't inspect them when you receive them.

The second area is 'in-process inspection'. Your procedures should specify how the inspection takes place. You need to know what quality problems can take place, and this will determine what checks you carry out. If your work has several stages, you may need to monitor each stage.

Service companies have processes just like a manufacturer, whether you manage an airport or provide accountancy services. Look back at the diagram that you drew of your work process. Where would you need to check that no mistakes have been made? Put a large 'C' in the relevant places.

Lastly, there is the 'final inspection'. This is the check you do when your work is complete and the product is about to be delivered to the customer. Have all the previous checks been done? For the airport manager, has the aircraft been completely serviced? For the accountant, do the numbers add up? Final inspection is usually done by reviewing all the records.

You might like to consider what tests or inspection you need to carry out on your product or service.

Inspection equipment

ISO 9000 goes into more detail on the subject of inspection equipment than virtually any other clause. The clause worries about your use of inaccurate measuring equipment. That is important if you manufacture precision items (the military needs to drop bombs in the right places).

The point of this clause is that if your micrometer is incorrect, everything you make will be outside your customer's specification. That would render your entire quality system quite useless. So you should not measure anything with an instrument of unknown accuracy.

Calibration is not needed for equipment which is used only for indication purposes (such as the temperature of a cooker in the kitchens). Some companies decide that only equipment used at final inspection needs to be calibrated against a national standard (see below). You do this by using a NAMAS laboratory; Appendix 3 has more details.

Tip

If you use non-calibrated equipment in the process and label the equipment as such, you avoid the expense of calibration tests.

Many service companies need to ensure that their test equipment works. For example, an electrical contractor needs to check that his meters are accurate, if he wants to avoid burning down the client's house. But for a purely service company, like a public relations consultancy, the clause is best ignored.

What is a national standard?

If you buy ten metres of wire, you want the shop to measure the length accurately, and not give you only 9.5 metres.

In the UK, the National Physical Laboratory maintains the standards for international units of length, mass and time. In other words, it has a metre rule against which all other rulers are compared.

Here are just a few areas of measurement which have national and international calibration standards:

Temperature	Electrical measurement
Hardness	Fluid measurements, such as flow of liquids and gases, pressure and density
Chemical analysis	Mechanical measurements, such as angle, form, volume and force.

There are also many industry standard tests. They measure things like the protective ability of face masks, the accuracy of colour measurement (useful for textiles companies), or even the testing of race horses for doping.

Many standards have a BS, EN or ISO number; NAMAS laboratories can check your measurements for accuracy against the relevant standard.

Now is a good time to ask yourself what the relevant measurements for *your* organisation are.

Inspection and test status

Can you demonstrate that your product has passed its various checks? Manufacturing companies would normally have a routing card or a label, while a service company would keep a paper record.

Tip

Some companies only label rejects. This is management by exception. The same applies in storing products. If a product is on a specific shelf, it has passed inspection.

Service companies have several stages in their process. For example, a conference organiser would need to know the stage that a client's project had reached, from initial confirmation by the client, to booking the venue, organising the speeches and slides, and getting paid.

Fill in the box below with your key stages and your checking procedures for each one.

Table 8.2 Key stages and checking procedures

What are the key stages of our process?	How can we demonstrate that our product has been checked at each of these stages?

Taking action when things go wrong

There are four things you can do with products that are not right.

1. **You can re-work it** – If too much of your output has to be re-done, it is worth instituting your corrective action procedure, to see how the problem can be resolved. Re-work applies in many service businesses, where a report has to be re-written, or a new computer network fails to work.

2. **You can decide that it is acceptable** – This is where some battles take place between inspection staff (who declare that the product is of poor quality) and the production people (who insist that it is fine).

3. **You can re-grade it** – There is a thriving industry built upon selling

'seconds' of crockery, shoes and textiles. Many factories earn good revenue from selling their downgraded goods to people eager to snap up a bargain. Companies which sell pure services are unlikely to have this option, but a steel company can upgrade its steel while a courier company can offer to charge the customer less for a delayed package.

4. **You can scrap it** – Some products are so badly made that you have to start again. In a company making plastic pipes, the poor quality piping produced at the beginning of a production run is simply melted down and used as raw material, with no waste being produced. (However, extra cost is incurred as a result of not getting the product right first time).

These four principles apply equally to service organisations, especially where the customer complains (like a diner complaining that his meal is cold). I once worked in a butcher's shop, where I had to mince some beef. Unfortunately, I set the controls wrong. The beef became so finely minced that it resembled porridge. The butcher had four choices:

1. he could re-work it (putting it back through the machine to make it look like mince);
2. he could put it on sale;
3. he could offer it at a discount, or
4. he could throw it away.

The butcher chose 1. He made the beef look like mince again, and then put it on sale without comment. Later I accidentally minced a plastic spoon into the beef. The butcher decided to scrap this.

In a service business, 'non-conformance' often means that the client has complained about the work. The company needs a plan for dealing with this kind of incident.

Case history: The house that vanished

Elizabeth and her husband Andrew paid a deposit on a new house in a desirable new development. At the time, the site was just a field. But the builder had an excellent reputation.

Elizabeth went to the site nearly every day to watch her house taking shape. Soon the foundations were laid and the first floor was built. Not long after, the house got its second floor. It only needed a roof to make it look like a real house.

One day, Elizabeth arrived as usual, only to find her house had disappeared. There was a hole in the ground where it had been.

The previous night, the builder's quality control people had found that the house was ten centimetres too short. The company had bulldozed the house and started again.

Elizabeth was astonished. She and her husband had sold their house, and were living in temporary accommodation. It was going to take months to re-build her house.

The company's marketing department, which had not been told of the planned demolition, were equally upset. They thought that the couple would have accepted the house, despite its 10cm shortfall, providing they were given a suitable discount.

In other words, the house could have been re-graded rather than scrapped. This would have satisfied the customers who were desperate to move in, and would have saved a lot of money.

In the end, the couple told the newspapers, which gave extensive coverage to the house that disappeared.

HANDLING AND STORING YOUR PRODUCT

The standard says you must handle, store, pack and deliver your product in such a way that it isn't damaged.

You need rules to govern the way that your staff handle and protect the product during processing, and as it moves through the plant.

Assessors like to see that you have a warehouse for your finished product (and stores for holding half-finished product while between processes). Woe betide you if your workforce puts boxes on the floor or leaves cartons in passages.

For service companies, handling is important where you have something perishable, like food.

Likewise, electricity and telephone companies have large amounts of equipment and material which needs to be carefully looked after.

ENHANCED SERVICING

By now, you have delivered your product to the customer. All that remains is to keep the customer happy. For ISO 9000, this means Servicing (clause 4.19). It is one of the briefest clauses. It suggests, rather diffidently, that if you provide servicing, you should write down the way you do it, and make sure it happens.

For manufacturers who produce goods that contain motors or use power (whether kettles, cars or cranes), servicing is a fundamental part of the business. Documented procedures will be useful.

Many service companies also provide servicing. A fuel supply firm may service boilers, an equipment retailer may service office equipment, and an architectural practice may supervise the construction of the building it designed.

SUMMARY

- 'Contract review' means checking the order. You should check that you can meet the customer's needs.
- To implement 'process control', you have to understand in detail how your organisation works. Use this opportunity to make the work flow more smoothly.
- Check whether you have any 'special processes'. Those are ones that can't be checked once they have been carried out.
- ISO 9000 asks you to inspect goods when you receive them, while you are processing them, and when you have finished processing them. This isn't always applicable to a service business.
- Any measuring equipment used for final inspection should be checked against a national standard.
- You should be able to tell whether any product has passed all its tests.
- When you identify faulty products, you should take the appropriate action, and record the decision.
- You have to handle and store your products properly, and have written procedures for this.
- Servicing needs to be controlled.

9

HELPING YOUR STAFF PERFORM BETTER

$$\blacklozenge$$

In this chapter, you'll learn about:

■ Defining people's roles.

■ Choosing a quality manager.

■ Involving top management in managing the system.

■ Training and communication.

DEFINING PEOPLE'S ROLES

You need to identify the people who are responsible for quality.
There are two ways you could do this:

1. Have an organisation chart showing how departments relate to each other, and how jobs in each department are structured. An example is shown in Figure 9.1.

2. Provide job descriptions for all managers and senior technical staff. A detailed job description could include:

 - the job title;
 - purpose of the job (reasons why this job is necessary);
 - job grade (seniority in the organisation)
 - location (which department, and whether travel is needed);
 - responsibilities (what the employee has to do);
 - authority (actions which the employee can take);
 - reporting to (the manager to whom the employee reports);
 - responsible for (employees who report to this job title);

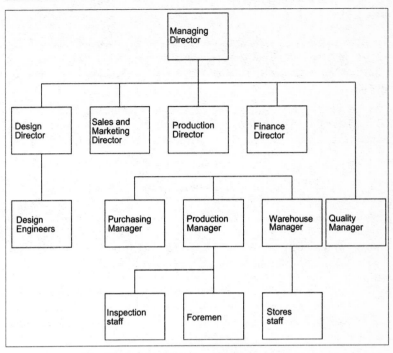

Figure 9.1 An organisation chart

- targets (the employee's goals);
- conditions (for example, whether the employee needs a driving licence).

A job description ensures that everyone knows what they are responsible for by including all their tasks. It will prevent unnecessary conflict between individuals and departments.

Some management gurus don't like job descriptions because they create demarcations and discourage initiative. This may be true, but there are benefits in ensuring that people know what their job is.

Setting job descriptions can result in people losing roles which they are used to playing. Others will be given added responsibilities. Some people may become more senior, while others seem to be demoted. This is a difficult period of time, and people must be handled sensitively. But there are benefits in sorting out all the inconsistencies and clarifying people's roles. You may find that some long-serving employees have been drawing a salary without serving a purpose.

Tip

Job descriptions aren't absolutely essential. ISO 9000 (BS 5750) merely asks to identify who is responsible for quality, and what their relationship with each other is. An organisation chart will usually suffice.

In a consultancy, for example, the client should be told in writing who is responsible for the assignment, and who is supervising the consultants. The consultants themselves should be told who has overall responsibility for the work.

CHOOSING A QUALITY MANAGER

You have to choose the quality manager carefully. The manufacturing company that appoints a tired old inspection manager to do the job is unlikely to develop an effective QA system. Old habits die hard, and the new manager will continue to run an inspection-based quality control system.

Some consultants believe that the quality manager should be very familiar with the company's processes. This has merits, because he is unlikely to try and impose alien systems on the company. In one case, the chief executive read the Standard and then, without anyone's help or guidance, implemented a very effective system. So in-depth knowledge helps.

Experience of other companies' quality systems is a major advantage, if only because it gives you examples of good and bad practice. This is an argument for hiring an outsider. But if the new quality manager comes from outside the business, and has preconceptions about how the system should work, he could create difficulties for the business.

The quality manager needs to be analytical: he has to be able to isolate the causes of faults. He also has to be interested in detail. He has to enjoy the often microscopic detail that quality assurance requires. There is no room for sloppiness or vagueness in managing quality.

Above all, the quality manager should be able to work with people. Other than wielding the ultimate threat ('I'll tell the Chief Executive'), he is powerless. He cannot usually force production people to do something they don't want to do. He can only motivate them and guide them. And he has to gain their agreement on how faults will be tackled.

THE WORK OF THE QUALITY MANAGER

The quality manager's work is as follows:

■   To guide managers in designing and setting up the quality system.

- To ensure that the quality system is maintained.
- To ensure that procedures are written for all main processes.
- To ensure that faults and complaints are resolved.
- To issue updated documents and ensure that old copies are withdrawn.
- To check that procedures are kept up to date.
- To ensure that audits and other checks are properly carried out. To check the results of the audits, and make sure that faults are rectified.
- To find out why faults occur, using statistics if necessary.
- To meet with senior management to decide what should be done about quality failings. To suggest how quality can be improved.

The quality manager's responsibilities *do not* include things like writing work instructions, carrying out audits, or rectifying faults. This is the job of line management, as we see next. Likewise, the quality manager should not have to approve documents (otherwise he will spend his life signing forms). Line management can do this.

INVOLVING TOP MANAGEMENT IN MANAGING THE SYSTEM

ISO 9000 requires senior management to check that the quality system is working properly (clause 4.1.3). This is generally done in a quality review meeting, though it can be simply an agenda item at a management meeting.

The meeting is attended by the board member responsible for quality and the quality manager (if he is a different person). Line managers with special responsibility for quality (for example, production managers) should also attend. Other people may be asked to attend for specific parts of a meeting (for example, the warehouse manager would need to sit in the meeting if a quality problem has occurred in the warehouse).

A certification body will expect to see that the reviews are held at least annually. In practice, customers won't wait a year for improvements to be made. Quarterly meetings may be better, with monthly meetings in the first year of the system. If a particular quality problem arises, you may want to hold an emergency review meeting.

The review needs to be effective. This means minuting the results of each review, and circulating them to relevant managers.

The quality manager needs to ensure that any changes required by the review team are put into practice. Each review meeting should check a list of previous action points, to ensure that the changes have been made.

The topics for discussion are shown in Table 9.1. They include:

Audits – The results of internal audits should feed into the review meeting, with the quality manager indicating how defects should be corrected. This loop should be completed by having the relevant department manager take action to prevent the defect from recurring.

When you first implement ISO 9000, achieving change through audits will help you improve your process. It will also be important to resolve any non-conformances that the certification body discovers: your certificate may depend on your rectifying these problems.

Complaints or customer feedback – As discussed in *Seductive Selling* (Kogan Page), quality of customer service is all that distinguishes companies in many markets. So you must take customer complaints or comments seriously.

New legislation – If new laws or standards relating to the workplace are introduced, the meeting would be the place to consider them.

The market – Quality systems can easily become too inward looking. To avoid this happening, the review should consider any developments in the outside world. This might include changes to business practice, or developments in quality thinking.

Table 9.1 Contents of the management review

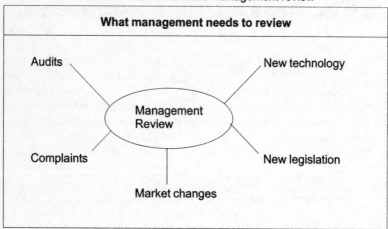

TRAINING AND COMMUNICATION

Product quality depends on the knowledge of your staff. It is often human beings who make errors, not machines. So training is important.

You should identify the training that people need to do their job. Then you have to provide the appropriate training. Finally, you have to keep training records. Assessors like asking to see training records.

You might need to provide training on:

- Technical or vocational skills (such as teaching people how to assemble a product, or sending them to college to learn electronic engineering). Staff should be supervised until they are competent to carry out their tasks.
- Human resource training (such as team working or leadership).
- Quality system training (how to use or manage the quality system).

When training staff to use ISO 9000, you need to explain why you have introduced the system, and how to use it. If you don't, staff are less likely to use the system.

Auditors need to know how to audit the system. And managers need to understand the nature of the new system they are supposed to manage. If staff think their manager does not understand ISO 9000 or believe in it, they won't implement it.

Tell staff why you are seeking registration, and what it involves. Try to explain what benefits *they* will get from it.

Case history: Lack of training makes a quality failure worse.

Britain's leading domestic appliance manufacturer sent one of its 2000 field service engineers to repair a dishwasher. The machine was a kind that he had never seen before, being from a firm which the company had just taken over.

Equipped with only a manual, he opened up the dishwasher. Several parts seemed to be missing from the machine. He had been given a part to fit, but there seemed to be nowhere he could fit it.

The customer, already angry with the new machine's failure, was made angrier still by the repair man's failure to mend the dishwasher. This was caused by a lack of training.

Training can take many forms, from a one-hour seminar by the departmental manager to an evening course at a local college. Some courses which have been developed by the Institute of Quality Assurance (see Appendix 3) lead to a recognised qualification, such as Lead Auditor.

You might like to consider the kinds of training your staff need.

Explain the system to all staff

Don't forget to include freelance staff, those who work on a part-time or seasonal basis, holiday workers and temps. These are the very people who

will be less familiar with how you do things, and so they are more likely to
make mistakes.

Out-workers and people who work from home are also more difficult to
control. They may need special training, since they work without supervision.

An initial meeting

Some companies start their ISO 9000 programme by holding a meeting for
managers. Here they explain the system and answer questions. This is an
efficient way of ensuring that everyone hears the same message at the same
time. They can then disseminate the information to their staff.

But there are disadvantages to this method. You only need one or two
vocal dissenters, and the very future of your standard is in doubt. The
meeting can end up as an argument between you and the rest of the
managers.

It may be better to meet managers individually. Your first visits should
be to those who are most likely to oppose it. Typically, they could be:

■ Longstanding employees (who will say, 'Why do we need to change?
  Our ways are tried and tested'.)
■ Those who operate in a fire-fighting manner. They thrive on crisis, and
  will try to prove that there are no systems relevant to the sort of work
  they do.
■ Those who operate without disciplines. They will feel the need to be
  unshackled. They will see ISO 9000 as inflexible and bureaucratic.
■ Those who work in creative jobs.

Get them involved. Seek their advice. Explain to them the advantages of the
system (which are shown in Chapter 3). Explain how the system will make
their job easier. Accept that there will be some disadvantages, too. If they
are used to working without any disciplines, or to operating in a fire fighting
mode, you will have to explain the benefits of planning and systems.

Adopt a friendly and persuasive approach to your colleagues. Encourage
them to participate in developing the system. Let them take ownership of
the system and especially their part of it. A production manager should be
in control of his plant, and that includes the systems which make it work.

Tip

Offer a prize to the department which is first to finish writing its
procedures. The prize could be a box of chocolates – Quality Street,
of course.

Other methods of communication

If you initially had difficulty understanding how ISO 9000 worked, imagine the problems your workforce will have.

So you will have to put effort into communication. Some firms produce a booklet which explains how ISO 9000 works. Others put articles about ISO 9000 in their newsletter. Some issue a regular ISO 9000 newsletter.

A newsletter demonstrates the company's commitment to the standard. It also tells people who may be scattered in different departments how other parts of the business are tackling the Standard.

The best newsletters give examples of how ISO 9000 is helping staff to do a better job. They share the problems and frustrations of those who are implementing the Standard.

Style of communication

However you communicate, avoid the tortuous language of the Standard. ISO 9000 is so complicated that you have to work extra hard when it comes to communication. Use short sentences and simple words.

What you say is equally important. There is no benefit in exhorting people to implement the system, still less to 'get it right first time'. Don't harangue people. What they need is *useful information*. Build awareness of ISO 9000. Find out what problems people have, and use the newsletter to answer them.

Explain how ISO 9000 works (in simple terms, with no jargon). Use departmental case histories to celebrate successes or discuss concerns. Above all, keep the tone cheerful, even light-hearted.

As the project proceeds, people will have different information needs. In the beginning, they will want to know whether ISO 9000 will make them redundant or make life difficult for them. Towards the end, they will have detailed questions about implementing certain procedures.

Avoid slogans and posters

It is all too easy to put up posters proclaiming 'quality is everyone's responsibility'.

The workforce ignore slogans. Your staff will be waiting to see whether the posters simply mean 'work harder', or 'we'll blame you for quality problems'.

The staff will want to know if you have a real commitment to quality. They know how to improve quality. They know it means training people, not simply hiring people straight from school and putting them to work. They know it means investing in machines which don't keep breaking down. They know it means listening to people's suggestions, and acting upon them.

They know it means better communication – management telling people what's going to happen and why it's happening.

If your organisation takes the standard seriously, ISO 9000 will be a watershed in its history.

SUMMARY

- You need to define people's responsibilities. This usually means having an organisation chart, and possibly job descriptions.
- It is important to choose a quality manager who understands how to create a quality system. Ideally, he should understand your business.
- You need to hold a regular quality meeting with someone from senior management. The meeting will examine any problems that have been found in the quality system, and agree changes.
- ISO 9000 requires you to give jobs only to properly trained people. You need to identify what training they need.
- You should decide how to explain ISO 9000 to staff. Consider a staff meeting, newsletters or a booklet.
- Ensure that you give people useful information, not slogans.

10

CONTROLLING YOUR SYSTEM

◆ ———————

In this chapter, you'll learn about:

■ The benefits of controlling important documents.

■ Only including what you must.

■ Learning from your mistakes.

THE BENEFITS OF CONTROLLING IMPORTANT DOCUMENTS

One of the major reasons for faults, especially in manufacturing, is that people are working from old versions of drawings or work instructions.

Another fault occurs when people start informally to modify the way things are made, often making pencilled notes on the work instructions. This can result in errors.

So it is important to make sure that everyone has up to date copies, and that previous copies are taken out of circulation. This ensures that 'everyone is singing from the same hymn sheet'. It is really a matter of good communications. If everyone is made aware of changes, fewer errors will be made. ISO 9000 (BS 5750) provides a structure for this, called Document Control.

You control the vital documents of your quality system, particularly the procedures that describe your work process and your system.

These become controlled documents. ISO 9000 asks you to specify how these documents will be distributed, and how they will be updated. Try to keep the number of controlled documents to a minimum; too much paper creates a burdensome system.

You need to take special care about updating the documents. The changes have to be formally agreed by someone who approved the old version, or who understands the process. Then the new version has to be formally issued, and the old copies collected.

All other documents (including informal and unnumbered copies of controlled documents) are called *uncontrolled* . That means they don't have to be audited or checked. They are not part of the quality system. Staff should not use them in their work.

With photocopiers everywhere, it is easy for people to make copies of a work instruction. They take these copies to a meeting or give them to a supplier. It is important to discourage the internal use of uncontrolled copies of documents. Imagine that someone takes a photocopy of a superseded drawing, and leaves it on a workbench. Another person comes along, looking for information, finds the drawing, and starts working from it. It is bound to lead to faulty material.

Setting up a document control system

When you set up your quality system, you will have to decide which documents are to be controlled. You should give each procedure a unique number, and possibly a date of issue. Pages should be numbered as 'Page 1 of 6', so that people know if any pages are missing.

Tip

To aid clarity, put a block or a strip of text at the top or bottom of each sheet of each controlled document. This will show the document number, date of issue and page number. A word processor can do most of this automatically.

You should also decide who should be on the circulation list for different manuals, and a master list should show who gets copies of the manual.

Not everyone needs the full manual. Only give people what they need to know. Don't send copies to departments that are not part of the quality system. If those staff open the manual, they won't understand what it means, and it will make them hostile towards the system. Similarly, only send to the purchasing department the sections of the manual that deal with purchasing.

Tip

Have as few controlled documents as possible, and avoid issuing

more than you need. This will reduce your administrative burden and make it easier to control the documents.

Updating the procedures

The quality manager should regularly check with the various departments whether controlled documents need to be revised. Revisions come about because of product improvements or alterations, because new products are created, or to rectify errors.

Once the revision has been agreed with authorized personnel (normally the departmental manager), the quality manager issues the revised procedure. This will carry a new number or a new date. Accompanying the new procedure will be a memo asking for the recipient's signature confirming that he has received the new instruction, and asking for the return of the old one.

Using a common format

Your procedures should have a similar format and layout, to aid understanding. People will be able to understand other departments' procedures; and using a standard format helps people to include all the relevant information. A procedure will usually include the following headings:

Responsibility
The job title of the person with the responsibility of ensuring that the procedure is carried out.

References
You may include a reference to the ISO 9000 clause number to which the procedure relates. You might also refer to other documents or records mentioned in the procedure.

The procedure
This is the instruction itself. It says how the work should be carried out.

ONLY INCLUDE WHAT YOU MUST

Be careful about including every word of the Standard into your manual.

For example, clause 4.6.3 of the Standard talks about including on your purchase orders the grade of material required. But look closely at the clause, and you will see the words 'where applicable'. If you feel that it is not applicable to specify the grade of material in your purchase order, you don't have to do so (assuming, of course, that your case is reasonable).

Throughout ISO 9000 there are little weasel words which distinguish what you *must* do from you *may choose* to do. If the Standard says that you *shall* do something, you have to do what it says. But here are some examples of clauses that you may not have to implement:

Timely consideration shall be given to the following activities...
Where appropriate, ...
... by means of measures such as ...
Where practicable, ...
Where applicable, ...
Where specified in the contract, ...
... as necessary...

The same is true for parts of the Standard that do not apply to your organisation. You do not have to implement them. A service business, for example, could waste a lot of time worrying about packaging, when it is not relevant.

Tip

State in the manual which clauses or activities you have excluded from your system. This will prevent the assessor from assuming you have accidentally omitted them. For example, you may not have test equipment (clause 4.11).

Case history: Building an ISO 9000 system that fits

Murphy is a £150 million civil engineering and construction company with clear ideas on how to implement ISO 9000. 'We don't have work instructions telling a surveyor how to set up a theodolite', says Val Harris, its Quality Manager. 'We expect them to know these things.'

'Nor do we calibrate every tape measure in the business. The construction industry operates under unpredictable conditions, so normally there is no point in setting the sorts of tolerances found in more controlled situations like phrmaceuticals or aerospace.'

At one time the company's quality manual was a huge tome. Now the company has condensed it into a slim volume. 'I've cut the unnecessary verbiage and taken out the forms to reduce the bulk,' says Val. 'I even use double-sided photocopying to make it look slimmer.'

The Murphy Group has also reduced the complexity of each procedure. 'Some companies' procedures have pages of introductory words. They put off the reader, and make the procedure harder to understand.'

Val always personally accompanies any visiting assessor. 'Our staff understand their own jargon,' he says, 'but not necessarily the assessor's quality jargon. It's part of my job to translate the assessor's questions.'

'I've also abandoned the words "Quality Assurance". To many people, it means a vast paperwork exercise. Now I just talk about "quality". I'd even like to get rid of the word "quality", too, because it has unhelpful meanings for some people. But we haven't yet found a word to replace it.'

'ISO 9000 is common-sense management,' he says. 'It isn't something to be afraid of. For years we'd done most of what ISO 9000 requires, only now we've documented it. That gives us greater control, and ensures that everyone knows what is expected of them.'

Quality plans: an aid to better information

Some companies have projects rather than a production line. The project might involve constructing a tunnel, assembling a batch of electronic goods to a client's specification, or installing a new computer system.

In a case like this, the company may produce a quality plan for each project. The quality plan demonstrates to the client that the project is properly controlled. The plan should be available on-site for the duration of the project, and it should answer the following questions:

■ What activities are to take place during the contract? This will list the sequence of actions. For example, one of them might be 'Machining'.

■ How will you carry out each activity? This will usually be a reference to a procedure number (in this case the machining procedure).

■ To what standard will the work be carried out? What are the acceptance criteria? In the case of machining, the work would need to be accurate to the relevant drawing.

■ How do you know that the work has been done? What records will be kept? In this case, it might be a route card. Stamps and reports are also used as verifying methods. The client may be asked to sign his acceptance of some or all stages of the work.

For companies with ISO 9000, the quality plan can be a specific part of the quality system. For companies which don't have ISO 9000, the quality plan can be a precursor to implementing the standard. But quality plans are normally restricted to large and expensive projects that take months or even years to complete. ISO 9000 does not oblige you to have a quality plan.

LEARNING FROM YOUR MISTAKES

As Figure 10.1 shows, there are lots of ways that you find out about problems. You may make a batch of defective products. Internal audits may find that a particular procedure is not being used. Customers may ring up and complain.

You need to take action to remedy these problems. If you don't take action, the problems will keep recurring.

If your tyres are bald, you need to get them replaced. If you don't, you'll have a series of near misses, followed by an accident. Once established, problems don't go away. They remain until someone fixes them.

Yet in some businesses, you can hear people say, 'We've had that problem for years'. Corrective action really means learning from your mistakes.

If you have field service engineers, are they constantly fixing the same problems? They, more than anyone, know what is wrong with your product. But does any one listen to them? Does anyone systematically analyse their reports?

With preventative and corrective action, you iron problems out of the system. But corrective action requires energy and commitment. Often it's simpler just to fix the machine or re-do the paperwork than look for the causes behind the problems. People get bogged down with their work, so it is difficult for them to see beyond their immediate problems. Corrective action is likely to involve other departments and people who will disagree with your diagnosis or feel defensive about their work.

Yet corrective actions are almost always simple things, and people on the shop floor often know what needs to be done. You can even ask your customers, 'What do we do wrong? What would you prefer us to do differently?'

You also find opportunities for improvement. These opportunities are revealed in audits or by staff suggestions. Companies like Procter and Gamble have customer care lines which get calls from thousands of consumers every year.

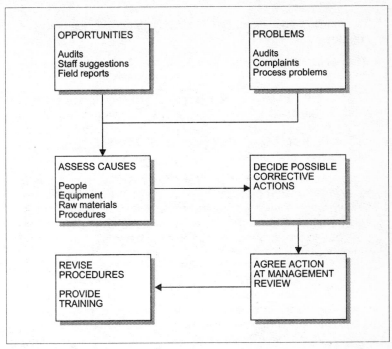

Figure 10.1 Taking corrective action

Case history: How a quality programme brought hidden problems to light for an electricity company.

When Northern Electric introduced a quality programme, its staff identified many problems which needed correcting. Here are a few of them:

Shortage of stationery for computer billing runs.

Ring spanner unsuitable for ABC connectors

Difficulties in reading alterations on claim forms.

Shortage of waste bottles for laser printers.

Too many queries from creditors.

Staywire drums too heavy.

Regular shortages of materials.

Incorrect meters specified on documents.

The company saved £2000 a year simply by raising a skip 4cms. Vehicles bringing in surplus clay after trench digging tipped the waste into a skip. But because the towball was catching the side of the skip, half of it ended on the ground. Raising the skip solved the problem, and saved the cost of clearing up the mess.

In another part of the company, staff were walking past ringing telephones. When the calls were answered, they were sometimes wrongly routed. Following brainstorming, a new procedure was introduced. Call errors in one section have now fallen from 13 a day to three. Customer complaints have dropped from 60 a month to seven.

You should assess the cause of each problem. Perhaps the procedure has been wrongly written or is out of date? Having selected the best corrective action, the quality manager will make his report at the Management Review meeting. Change is brought about by revising the relevant procedure, by undertaking training, or some other corrective action.

It's easy to see when a product is at fault, but more difficult to define problems with *service* delivery. At St Joseph's and St Teresa's school, there were 'rush hour' problems. Every morning, there was congestion in the corridors, and the smaller children were in some danger of being hurt. The head teacher decided to make some changes.

She decided that the children would line up in the playground near their respective classes, and would be escorted, a class at a time, to their classroom. In this way she identified a problem and took corrective action.

She has probably never heard of ISO 9000, but she took further steps of which a quality manager would approve. She documented the new procedure in writing, communicated it to staff, children and teachers, and now carries out periodic audits. This entails her standing in the playground to check that the system is working. Is it a wonder that parents are queuing to get their children into her school?

Look at the examples of quality failures you wrote in Chapter 1. What corrective action can you take to prevent them from happening? Put your solutions in the box below.

Table 10.1 Preventing mistakes from recurring

Corrective action our organisation can take

SUMMARY

- Important documents, especially your procedures, need to be controlled, so that everyone uses the current version.
- These documents should only be handed out on a 'need to know' basis.
- Only include elements of the Standard that are essential to your business. Many parts of the Standard are optional.
- A quality plan is sometimes used to control large projects. It tells staff and the client how the job will progress.
- If you find things going wrong, you should take action to resolve them. Corrective action is one of the most valuable parts of ISO 9000, because it helps you resolve complaints and other symptoms of failure.

11

HOW TO AUDIT

In this chapter, you will learn about:

- The three main kinds of audit.
- How to select internal auditors.
- How to set up an audit plan.
- How to carry out an audit.

THE THREE MAIN TYPES OF AUDIT

There are three types of quality audit: internal audits, supplier audits, and assessments. These are sometimes known as first, second and third party audits.

In this book we are mainly concerned with *internal audits*. An internal audit is carried out by your own staff, and it examines your own system. It is what ISO 9000 requires in clause 4.17. Some people call it a *first party audit*. The internal audit gives management the information it needs to make changes. The workforce should welcome it because it lets them tell management what changes should be made.

You carry out a *supplier audit* when you audit one of your suppliers. And one of your customers may visit your plant to check *your* quality. That, too, is a supplier audit. It is sometimes called a *second party* audit. Second party audits have a commercial link: a customer is assessing the quality of a supplier.

Tip

When you get tired of other people examining your system and criticising it, go and audit one of your suppliers. It is therapeutic to see them hoping you won't find problems. For a day, you can be as god-like and officious as any certification body. Ask probing questions, and demand to see inside cupboards. It will make you feel better.

Assessments are what happen when a certification body assesses you for ISO 9000. They also take place when you undergo a surveillance visit. These are often called *third party audits* . In Chapter 13 we look at what happens when a certification body comes to assess you. In the meantime, we focus on the internal audit.

Purpose of the internal audit

The internal audit serves several purposes:

- it checks to see whether the system is working properly, and whether there are any defects in the system;
- it looks for possible improvements;
- it discovers potential dangers or problems;
- it stops waste and loss;
- it checks that previously identified problems have been corrected.

To carry out the internal audit properly, you need to decide:

- who will perform the audit (see 'Selecting internal auditors', below);
- what they will examine (see 'How to set up an audit plan', below);
- to whom the results will be communicated (see 'When the internal audit is complete', below);
- how to make sure that any corrective actions are undertaken (see 'Correcting faults', below).

The assessor will look to see that you have written procedures to cover these points.

SELECTING INTERNAL AUDITORS

You will have to create and train a set of internal auditors. The number will depend of the size of your business. You could work it out by determining the number of work-hours it would take to audit every ISO 9000-certified process once a year. Then divide that number by the maximum number of work-hours you would want to spare an employee for auditing, and that gives you the number of auditors you need. Many companies select one auditor per department.

Internal auditors must not be involved in the process they are auditing (because that would make them biased). But they can work in the same department.

You should train your auditors to do the job professionally. This might mean sending them on an auditing course. There they will learn what to look for, what questions to ask, and how to identify non-conformances. In the UK, there is a training scheme called the National Registration Scheme for Assessors of Quality Systems (This also provides good training for quality managers).

The auditors don't need to have specialist knowledge of the process that is to be audited, though some understanding will be helpful. The auditors should understand what their auditing work entails: they must know what the manual requires, and they must check that it is being done.

HOW TO SET UP AN AUDIT PLAN

You have to demonstrate to the certification body that you carry out audits to a professional standard. That includes having an audit plan.

The certification body will expect to see a plan that looks like Table 11.1.

TABLE 11.1 An audit schedule

Internal Audit Schedule						
Area to be audited	Auditor	Scope of the audit	Report number	Sept	Oct	Nov etc
Purchasing	J Keynes	All activities	106	15		
Goods inward	A Smith	Records	107		6	
Manufacturing	N Lawson	All activities	108			22

The format shown in Table 11.1 has several features:

■ It tells you which departments are being audited and the activities to be audited.

■ The 'All activities' audits are likely to be a planned and routine audit. The records audit of 'Goods Inward' could be to check that errors identified in a previous audit have been sorted out.

■ The plan identifies the auditors, and the date (shown as a number).

■ It also provides a report number. This gives you a useful way of coding the audit reports.
■ This format can be used with a standard wall planner.

The audit plan is based on departments. This is logical because businesses tend to operate on a departmental basis. It follows that each department will have its own quality manual containing only the parts of the standard relevant to it.

Tip

Leave blank lines at the bottom of the plan so that you can do special audits when the need arises.

You may like to consider the areas you will need to audit. Remember to include all the departments covered by your quality system. Also include any parts of the system that are special to your organisation.

Correcting faults

How do you make sure that any errors you find get corrected? One way to do this is shown below. It is built into the audit plan, and expands on the diagonal lines shown in Table 11.1.

Table 11.2 Format for showing the status of audits

◹	Planned audit	–
◢	Audit undertaken	Non conformances found, action outstanding
◼	audit undertaken	Non conformances resolved
⊠	audit undertaken	No non-conformances

HOW TO CARRY OUT AN AUDIT

In the next section, we look at the difference between compliance and adequacy audits. We consider the timing of the audit, and how to ask the right questions. We also look at how to write non-conformance reports.

The adequacy audit

When you first set up your system, you will need to do an *adequacy* audit. This is to check your manual against the Standard. Does your manual meet the requirements of ISO 9000?

Where the Standard says you should keep supplier records, does your own manual state what records will be kept?

You do an adequacy audit by opening a copy of ISO 9000 at the first clause, and checking to see if your own manual contains the same clause. Do this methodically for every clause in the Standard. This is a job best done in peace and quiet, away from your firm. You'll find it useful to keep a table showing where in your manual each ISO 9000 clause is to be found.

It is a valuable exercise, because this will be the first action of your certification body. You can't get registered until your manual accurately reflects ISO 9000.

Assuming that your manual is adequate, you can now move on to a *compliance* audit. This checks whether people are doing what your manual says they should do. Here you are getting out and about, meeting the work force, and seeing what is going on. You should check to see whether:

- you have documented procedures for work which affects quality;
- those procedures are being carried out;
- records are being faithfully kept;
- people have been properly trained for their job.

Timing the audit

The best time to do an audit is when a department is at its busiest. That is when people take short-cuts, and mistakes are made. You might want to do an audit in the run-up to a peak selling period (perhaps early Spring), or on a day when people are not at their best (we've all heard of Friday afternoon cars).

Make sure that the auditee (the victim and his department) knows about the audit well in advance. You aren't trying to catch him out – you want his part of the system to work properly. If he can fix problems before you arrive, he is to be congratulated. And if you don't find major problems, show that you are pleased. An error-free audit means that everyone wins.

Most internal audits are planned up to a year ahead and are routine. But you may need to do an adhoc audit. It might result from a previous audit which had revealed a new kind of defect. It could stem from a customer's complaint. Or you might want to check that corrective action has been taken.

Many organisations use a management consultant to audit their quality system shortly before their initial assessment by the certification body. This has to be done early enough to allow the non-conformances to be communicated to staff, and corrective action taken. On one 'pre-assessment', a management consultancy was asked to do an audit just three days before the assessors arrived. This was leaving it rather late.

Have a checklist

A checklist is a good way of ensuring that all the right questions are asked. If the checklist is used to excess, it turns the auditor into a robot. The auditee will learn to give the 'right' answers like a clever chimpanzee.

The chief executive of one quarry company fends off customers' questionnaires by answering 'not applicable' to any questions he thinks he will fail. Customers cannot make much use of the questionnaires they send out, because none of them have noticed this.

Appendix 3 contains a general pre-assessment questionnaire that you could expand to cover individual departments. The trick is to reverse the wording of each clause. If a clause says:

> The supplier shall ensure that purchased product conforms to specified requirements

your checklist could ask:

> How do you ensure that purchased product conforms to specified requirements?

You could even ask:

> What *are* the specified requirements?

Questions to ask

If as an auditor you ask, 'Do you check your work?', the answer will be 'Yes'. Questions which seek a yes/no response do not get the fullest answer, nor the most truthful.

It is better to ask *open* questions. These require the person to reply with a sentence. Open questions start with who, what, where, why, when or, how.

Experienced auditors follow up the answer with the words, 'Show me'. This requires the auditee to point to a specific document or demonstrate an action. A variation on this is to ask, 'Can you show me how...?', or 'Can you explain how..?'

The way you tackle the audit

Audits must not be used to blame people. If people find that quality audits are used to attack them, you will get no co-operation.

What's more, the defects may not be the employee's fault. Maybe he hasn't been trained? Maybe no one has involved him in writing the procedure? Maybe the procedure is wrong, and he has a better way of working?

That is one advantage of audits. They can lead to great improvements, providing that everyone uses them positively. So from the very start you must make it plain that audits will not be used in a hostile way.

Tip

Give an award for an error-free internal audit. Auditors sometimes give less praise than they should. A department which gets through an internal audit with no major non-conformances deserves public recognition. This could be a verbal or written commendation, or a certificate for the department's wall.

Writing non-conformance reports

As Figure 11.1 shows, your audit may reveal no problems. But if you find a problem, you have to take corrective action. This is a topic we looked at

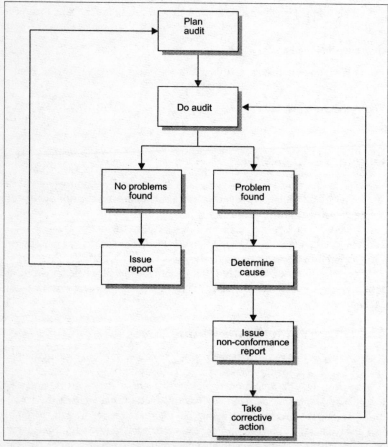

Figure 11.1 Auditing the system

NON-CONFORMANCE REPORT

Company: XYZ Co.   Audit No: 1932
Dept/Process: Quality   Date: 2 March 19XX
Auditor: J Keynes   Auditee: N Lawson, Quality
                                           Manager

Auditor's Observation

I found that no minutes of management reviews were available for the
last 12 months.

Observation Agreed – N. Lawson

This is a non-conformance against clause 4.1.3 of ISO 9001 which states
that records should be maintained

Signed: J Keynes   Date: 2 March 19XX

Proposed Corrective Action

Henceforth, management reviews will be minuted and distributed to
managers of all departments mentioned.

Signed: N. Lawson, Quality Manager   Date: 2 March 19XX

Review of corrective action

Minutes of management reviews are now being maintained.

Signed: N. Lawson, Quality Manager   Date: 4 April 19XX

Figure 11.2 A sample non-conformance report

in the previous chapter. You will have to decide what has caused the
problem, and this is usually obvious.

When you find defects, you should document them, and make sure they
get corrected. A form has evolved to help you do this. It is shown in Figure
11.2.

This non-conformance report shows you that J Keynes was auditing the
quality department, and discovered that there were no records of management reviews. Perhaps the quality manager, N Lawson, is so busy that he
is falling behind with his paperwork.

The non-conformance report is divided into three elements:

1. The auditor's report (which we will return to in a moment).
2. The proposed corrective action (N. Lawson promises to do better in
   future).
3. The review of corrective action (with N. Lawson noting that he has now
   started keeping minutes).

The auditor's report is worth dwelling on. The auditor has first made an *observation* . It simply says what he found. In some companies this is a finding, or even an opportunity to improve.

He then asked the person he is auditing (the quality manager) to agree that the observation was made. This ensures that the auditee cannot later deny that it happened.

The auditor then makes an *attribution* . This is a reference to the part of the manual or Standard that the fault contravenes.

When the internal audit is complete

You need to tell staff in the audited department about their non-conformances. Give them a copy of the non-conformance reports. There is no need to type them, unless you think they will be otherwise illegible. Sending them away for typing could add delays and costs to the system – always aim to avoid this.

Make sure that staff know how to remedy their failings. Suggest solutions. Ask staff exactly what steps they will take.

Agree the follow-up. This would be a meeting between the quality manager and the head of the department which has just been audited. At that meeting, you can go through the non-conformance reports, to see what action has been taken. If you wait until the next audit takes place, you could be delayed for 6 to 12 months, so an interim meeting is essential.

Some quality managers produce audit reports. These detail the objectives of the audit, the name of the department, date and so on. They may contain the names of people who were present at the audits or the meetings, the areas of non-conformance, the areas which were satisfactory, the people responsible for corrective action, and the time scale. If this format suits your business, use it. But it can become time-consuming.

SUMMARY

■ ISO 9000 expects you to organise internal quality audits. You will need to appoint internal auditors and arrange for an audit plan.

■ In addition, you will receive an assessment from your certification body. You may be audited by major customers and you may choose to audit your own suppliers.

■ Audits check whether the system is working properly, and whether improvements could be made. It also discovers potential dangers or problems. Any faults that are detected must be corrected.

■ You should communicate the results of the audit to relevant staff.

■ Non-conformance reports should be factual and brief.

12

BETTER INFORMATION

◆

In this chapter, you'll learn about:

■ Identifying and tracing your products.

■ The records you need to keep.

■ The advantages of keeping statistics.

■ Measuring the cost of quality failure.

IDENTIFYING YOUR PRODUCT

It's every company's nightmare. Some of your products are found to be unsafe, and have to be recalled. But which ones? If you can identify the faulty batches by their serial numbers, you can limit your losses.

The same holds true for smaller problems. If a customer complains about a product, you need to trace it back to the team that made it, or the supplier who produced the batch of raw material.

Large and costly items can each have a serial number. With smaller items, you should be able to identify a batch number.

Engineering companies often use a job card. A card accompanies each piece of work as it passes through the various processes. As it enters a new department, the operator has to sign that he has received the product in good condition. If he sees a flaw, it will be noted on the job card.

By using these methods, the company knows *who did what* to the product, and *what went where*. It ensures complete traceability.

Traceability is just as important in service businesses. If you install ventilating equipment, you need to know which installer put a system in. If a problem develops on one system, maybe the installer has incorrectly fitted the others he fitted? Or perhaps the product was at fault, in which case you might need to tell the other owners of that equipment?

Traceability is also important in the public sector. With increasing calls for open government, the public sector needs to encourage staff to be accountable for their work. The Social Services need to know who handled a particular case, and when, in case the decision is later queried.

Solicitors and other service organisations need to be able to trace the progress of correspondence with a customer, and to identify the actions taken. Each customer's account should have its own unique identification.

Tip

You can use bar codes to monitor your process from goods received to picking and shipping. Bar codes are now being used in the most unlikely situations. They are helping health organisations to monitor blood products, and track patients. They are also helping advertising agencies to check the progress of advertisement design and production.

Case history: Getting it right second time

Bright Plastic Panels sent a fitter to install some panels at a client's premises. He phoned his employers. 'The first panel is too *big*,' he said. 'It won't fit.' The factory told him to cut it to size.

Half an hour later, he was back on the phone again. 'The second piece is too *small*' he said. There was a pause at the other end of the line. The truth dawned. Both panels had been the right size. He had simply put each panel in the wrong place.

The firm had supplied a drawing, but as both panels were similar in appearance, the fitter had made a mistake. The company decided that in future it would number the panels on the back. In the meantime, it had to make a third panel to replace the one which was 'too small'.

This shows how important it is to identify your product and, when things go wrong, to take corrective action. It also reveals the costs associated with quality failures. The company had to make an extra panel, have it specially delivered, employ the fitter for twice the time needed, and lost a lot of management time.

KEEPING A RECORD

Keeping records is at the heart of ISO 9000 (BS 5750), and the assessor will try to find areas where your records are missing or out of date.

Once you have despatched your products, you have no way of proving that they were of the right quality, unless you keep records. Those records are your way of showing that you have a quality system in operation, and that your products are of the right standard.

It follows that you need records of the product checks you have made (inspection, as ISO 9000 calls it).

Some organisations keep records to monitor that production stays within set limits. As it starts to move outside those limits, production staff can take corrective action before defective goods start to be produced.

And if defective goods are produced, records will help you identify who produced them and when. This will help you take action to prevent problems recurring.

You also need minutes of meetings, such as design reviews or management reviews.

Audit records should be available, and there should be a master list to identify the location of copies of the quality manual.

Shown below in Table 12.1 are some of the records that you should keep to satisfy ISO 9000.

You can tell which ones are a requirement – they are noted in the Standard with the phrase 'see 4.16', this number being the clause about quality records.

Tip

The assessor won't ask to see records for any part of the standard which doesn't apply to your business. If you are a service business and you don't have any equipment which needs calibrating, you won't keep calibration records.

Table 12.1 The records you need to keep

Your work
Purchase orders, list of suppliers
Records of contract reviews
Minutes of design reviews
Inspection and test records
Records of accepted non-conforming products
Records of work done on special processes
Calibration records
Servicing records
Lost or damaged product which had been supplied by your customer

Your people	Your system	Your information
Training records	Records of procedures issued and revised	Records for tracing products
	Audit records	
	Corrective action taken	

Do you, like most companies, keep records on computer? If so, how will you ensure that the data is protected from corruption or loss in the event of a power failure? The assessor may look for back-up procedures.

Case history: a TV station that is about to go off the air

Television stations are full of cables. With thousands of wires, it is important to know which wire goes to which socket. This is what the engineers call 'cable scheduling'. Yet one UK television station operates without any records of its wiring.

The original wiring diagrams exist, but the engineers regularly make changes. 'We react to what the studios want,' said one engineer. 'We're supposed to document it. But it never gets beyond the back of a cigarette packet.'

All the cabling information is contained in the engineers' heads. The wiring is so complex that different engineers now understand only parts of their electronic system. It is a disaster waiting to happen.

There are three reasons for this. First, the entire station is so busy reacting to crises that the engineers don't have time to keep records. Secondly, the company does not have ISO 9000. Thirdly, it suits the engineers to have control of the station's output at a time of uncertainty over jobs.

LEARNING BY NUMBERS

Clause 4.20 talks about 'Statistical Techniques', which may seem a rather specialised branch of quality management.

The discussion about statistics is a nod in the direction of the quality gurus, in particular a man called Deming, who placed great reliance on statistics (Deming was a statistician).

But don't assume that you have to be a statistician to apply this clause. To get quality into your organisation, you have to communicate with the workforce and the managers. They will quickly switch off if you start talking about mean deviations. So your statistics should be simple ones.

The Japanese are great at statistics. They like to hang up large graphs in their factories. These graphs show how the business is doing. To a workforce used to being kept in the dark, this is a revelation.

What will you measure? A manufacturer will record the percentage of defective products produced, or the number of returns.

An airline can record the percentage of lost luggage, while a hospital can record the number of operations performed or its success rates in terms of life or death.

An assessor will expect you to specify the techniques you will use, when and where they will be used, and by which staff.

You might find it useful to make your own list of ways in which you can measure the quality of your service or product.

Measuring the cost of quality

One of the most valuable analyses you can do is to measure the cost of quality. This is the cost of doing things wrong. A reduction in the cost of quality will help you measure the success of your ISO 9000 programme over time. But the number of costs may grow as you get more experienced in measuring quality. So if you use it as a measure of progress, be prepared to re-work the cost of previous periods. Otherwise staff might think that their work is getting worse, the longer the quality programme lasts.

The cost of quality (or non-conformance, as it is also known) can be split into prevention, appraisal and failure costs. It is worth trying to estimate the total cost of quality. Seek the help of your financial department, and only include items which the department is prepared to verify.

As you learn more about the cost of quality, you may find that the cost of poor quality adds up to 25 per cent of your revenue. So if you only get to one or two per cent, you have probably missed some costs. Below are some items to include. You may find more of your own. Try to measure *your* cost of quality.

MEASURE YOUR COST OF QUALITY

- Prevention costs:
  - quality manager's salary;
  - internal audits;
  - cost of surveillance visits;
  - supplier assessments;
  - equipment maintenance costs;
  - meetings and management time connected with maintaining the quality system;
  - Quality training.
- Appraisal costs:
  - inspectors' salaries;
  - cost of staff time spent at goods inwards inspection, in-process inspection, and final inspection.
- Internal failure costs:
  - re-work and scrap;
  - waste disposal costs;
  - costs of re-design;
  - costs of re-inspection;
  - loss of revenue from downgrading.
- External failure costs:

— repairs under warranty;
— complaint handling (including sales force time, lost revenue or credit notes).
■ Total cost of quality (all the above).

The assessor will not ask you about your cost of quality, because it isn't part of ISO 9000. So you can safely ignore this topic. There *is*, however, a useful British Standard, BS 6143, on the subject.

Once you identify how much money is being wasted due to poor quality, you can target the areas for improvement. What is more, the cost of quality gets top management really interested.

Not every cost of quality is immediately obvious. The UK's Solicitor's Indemnity Fund reported a record number of claims in 1992 which required extra contributions from solicitors. The claims were mainly caused by simple errors; and only 10 per cent stemmed from a lack of legal knowledge. These errors cost the firms not just higher contributions, but also the lost revenue from dissatisfied clients.

Likewise, an Institute of Radiographers survey found 51 different possible ways of treating a hypothetical case of breast cancer. The lack of standardisation is putting extra costs on the hospitals which provide the treatment.

SUMMARY

■ You need to be able to identify your products, and trace them back to the people who made them. Traceability helps you rectify problems, and prevent them recurring.
■ ISO 9000 specifies the records that must be kept. These records should help your organisation be more effective.
■ You should decide which statistics you need to keep. These should not be overly complicated, and you should communicate them to your staff.
■ It is worth trying to assess the cost of quality. This will help to demonstrate the benefits of a good quality system.

13

GETTING REGISTERED

◆

In this chapter, you'll learn:

- How to choose a certification body.
- What happens during the assessment visit.
- Why companies seek registration.
- The reasons why companies fail.

HOW TO CHOOSE A CERTIFICATION BODY

Towards the end of the project, you invite an outside organisation (called a certification body) to assess your system. If the visit goes well, you get your certificate.

In Chapter 4 we had an initial look at certification bodies. You choose which one you want, and it is wise to treat them as you would any other supplier. As shown in Figure 13.1, you should ask several certification bodies to give you a quotation.

Some certification bodies are large multinational organisations. Their name may be internationally known, and this will be useful if you export. Other certification bodies concentrate on specific industries. For example, CARES works in the steel industry, PECS covers service businesses, and Trada specialises in the timber industry.

Ask the certification body if its 'scope of registration' includes your industry. In other words, does it have experience of working in your industry? Sources of information about certification bodies are given in Appendix 3.

The certification bodies will ask you to fill in a questionnaire. This asks about the number of your employees, the size of your site, and the nature of your work. It gives them an idea of the size of the task confronting them, and therefore how much work is involved.

The cost

The certification bodies will give you a price for doing the job. The price will be split into three areas:

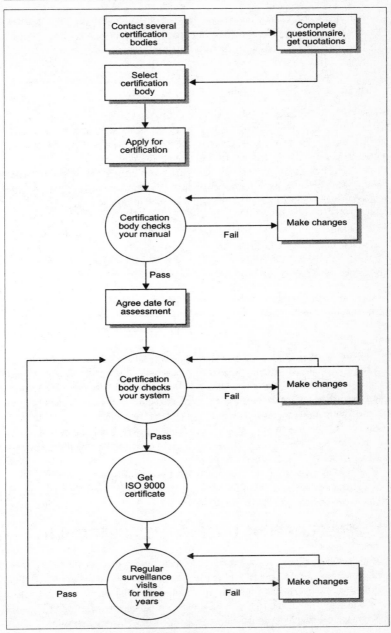

Figure 13.1 Getting your ISO 9000 certificate

1. The application fee. This covers the cost of processing your application, and setting up a plan for certifying you.
2. The assessment fee. This is for the time taken to visit your site and inspect your system.
3. Surveillance fees. These are the cost of visiting your site twice a year to check that you are maintaining your system.

Some certification bodies let you spread the cost over three years, which helps your cash flow by avoiding heavy initial costs. Some have a re-assessment fee every three years when they thoroughly re-inspect your business, while others don't. So it is worth comparing the costs.

The first person you meet from a certification body is likely to be a sales person, and he is unlikely to be the same person who turns up to do the assessment. So don't judge the organisation solely on the personality of the sales person.

With these thoughts in mind, you make your choice of certification body, and ask it to do an assessment.

Checking the manual

The certification body will first want to see your manual. It does this because your manual has to conform to the requirements of ISO 9000. In other words, if you don't even *claim* to be conforming to the standard, there is no point in having your site assessed.

If your manual fails, the certification body will point out the nature of the failings (what they call 'non-conformances'). They will ask you to tell them when you have made the changes. Bear in mind that they will expect to see that these changes have been made in practice as well as in the manual.

Once your manual passes the test, the certification body will want to visit your site, to see whether you are doing what your manual claims you do.

The date for assessment will approach at an ever increasing speed, as you realise all the things that need to be done.

If you find that some of your departments are simply not ready, try to delay the date of the assessment. Like a driving test, there is no point in undergoing the assessment before you are ready.

WHAT HAPPENS DURING THE ASSESSMENT

The assessor won't expect to see years of back data. So don't waste precious time, re-doing old documents. However, he will expect to see evidence that audits and management reviews have taken place, that document control is professionally managed, that you have written procedures for all your main processes, and that people do what the procedures say they should.

When he arrives, the assessor will go through a routine known in the trade as an opening meeting.

- He will introduce his colleagues (if your firm is large enough to need more than one assessor).
- He will confirm the areas to be covered and the purpose of the audit (to assess you for a certificate).
- He will tell you about major and minor non-conformances (see 'Types of non-conformance' below).
- He will ask for a guide. This could be the quality manager, or it could simply be an operative who knows his way around the site.
- He will check that there is an office which his team can use.
- He will want to check that the trades unions know of his arrival, so that the audit does not spark a 'walk-out'.
- He will tell you when he plans to report his findings (for example, at the end of the following day).

The assessor may also ask you, 'Is there anywhere you wouldn't want me to look?' This seemingly innocent question has two benefits for the assessor. If you say 'No, go ahead', he has the freedom to look anywhere he wants. If you say 'Yes', he will ask you why. You may have alerted him to an area of work that you have not included in your quality system.

At this point, the assessor will disappear with the guide, to start checking your system. This is a nail-biting time for the quality manager.

The assessor's method

The assessor will start by trying to understand how your business works. He may construct a flowchart, showing your process from Goods Inwards to Despatch.

He will then trace forward from the beginning of the process to the end, or work back in reverse. The assessor will visit all the departments which are involved with the Standard.

He will do spot checks in areas that experience tells him are weak spots on a company like your's. He will look at products, processes and documents. If your manual says you should check every batch, he might say, 'Show me the evidence that you checked every batch last Wednesday'.

He will ask to see your purchase order book, rifle through the leaves, and pull out an order at random. If your manual says you specify the size and shape, he will expect to see the specifications written on the order.

The assessor's checks

Your assessor could take any of the following actions. He might:

- Ask to see customer complaints. He will look to see if you have taken corrective action.
- Ask to see audit reports.
- Ask staff how they deal with a specific clause in the Standard
- Ask staff why they are performing a certain task, and to which written procedure it relates.
- Ask whether an instrument has been calibrated, and if so where the evidence is.
- Look for scrap, and check whether a non-conformance report was raised for it.
- Check whether drawings are registered, and are the current version.
- Ask management to explain how the quality system works.
- Ask staff about the quality policy.

The certification body may even know things about your business that you don't. Many certification bodies specialise in certain industries, and this gives them inside knowledge.

On being audited, one firm was surprised when the assessor asked, 'Can you tell me about a complaint made about you on 18 September by one of your trade customers, Jones Ltd?'

Hesitantly, the Quality Manager turned to his complaints book, and there sure enough, was a complaint by Jones Ltd for that day. It turned out that the assessor had certified Jones Ltd only a few days before, and had noticed its complaint among some paperwork.

So you shouldn't assume that by omitting an embarrassing record you can't be found out. Assessors have ways of learning the truth.

No one is perfect all the time, and the assessor will expect to see minor faults. Every time he sees something that you have failed to do, he will write out a non-conformance report. This will specify what he saw, which clause it failed to conform to, and why that was the case. A sample non-conformance report is shown in Figure 11.2.

The assessor will ask the guide to sign each non-conformance. In doing so, he is merely asking the guide to agree that they both saw an operator using a machine without guards, or that a box of finished products was lying in a passage way.

Types of non-conformance

There are two types of non-conformances: major and minor. A major non-conformance is one which affects the system. For example it might include failure to carry out a final inspection, or failure to document any procedures for your purchasing department.

In such cases, the certification body will refuse to give you a certificate.

Or as one certification body neatly puts it, 'For major non-conformities, corrective action must be completed prior to certification'.

A minor non-conformance is a single lapse which does not affect the system. It might be wrongly stored goods, or a batch that was not labelled. The assessor will expect to see a few non-conformances, and will not withhold your certificate for these lapses.

But if the assessor finds the same minor non-conformance in several departments (for example, a consistent failure to keep records), he might decide that it added up to a system failure, and would refuse to award you the certificate.

Case history: How certification led to new business for a rubber moulder

Founded in 1980, LVS Rubber Mouldings had by 1989 18 regular customers. It gained ISO 9000 in 1990, and by 1992 had expanded to 67 customers.

This growth was at a time of recession, when the company's automotive business shrunk by 10 per cent, hydraulics fell by 60 per cent, and pneumatics turnover fell by 40 per cent

It also helped the company win a major contract with NDM Manufacturing, part of Nippondenso, the world's largest automotive component manufacturer. 'We are the only UK supplier of rubber mouldings to this corporation,' said Cliff Holt, the company's General Manager. 'About 100 British firms were vetted, and we are the only one to achieve full quality approval. We were visited seven times by delegations of Japanese executives before contracts were signed.'

Dealing with the assessor

Roger Smith, Managing Director of BVQI, a certification body, says there is a generally accepted way of preparing your staff for assessment. It goes like this:

1. Think of ways you can delay the assessor.
2. Arrange lengthy lunches, ideally at a location as remote as possible from your organisation.
3. Do not answer any questions you have not been asked.
4. Hide any records that may be contentious or incomplete.
5. Get your assessors drunk if you possibly can.

This, he says, is not the best way to approach certification. If you believe in having a quality system, you should not need subterfuge. Assessors are experienced and know when something is going wrong.

One assessor noticed that when he passed a workshop cupboard, staff got visibly anxious. The cupboard was locked. He asked to see inside. The staff squirmed with anxiety. They begged him not to reveal what he was going to see. When they opened it, he saw half-mended lawnmowers and food mixers. This was where the staff mended their domestic equipment when no one was watching.

Assessors can vary

In an ideal world, all assessors would be highly experienced, intelligent, and trained so thoroughly that you would get consistent assessments. Sadly, this is not always the case. You may get different assessors every visit, and their calibre and attitudes can vary.

A client recently complained to its certification body about the low standards of its assessor. The client pointed out that he missed obvious non-conformances. You may think it strange for a client to demand that assessors be more rigorous.

But as the client pointed out, if the workforce feels no need to maintain the standard properly, the system will fall into disuse. The workforce needs to feel that retaining certification can only be achieved by keeping high standards. It needs to believe that the assessor will spot any non-conformances.

The closing meeting

At the end of the assessment, the assessor will tell you what non-conformances he found. Minor non-conformances will not prevent you from passing; but a major non-conformance will be a reason for failing.

By now you will have found that the assessor is a strange human being. He will be lacking in humour, and will not be interested in the normal pleasantries of life. At the closing meeting, he will refrain on commenting on the finely crafted procedures and the elegant structures you have put in place. Instead, he will solemnly list your failings, like an automaton. He may also give you hand-written pieces of paper containing all your non-conformances.

Do not accept the assessor's views in an unquestioning manner. He is, after all, an ordinary and fallible human being. Be prepared to refute any non-conformances if they seem unreasonable to you.

If you can get the assessor to downgrade a major non-conformance to a minor one, or even to drop it, it could make the difference between pass and failure.

Once the assessor has left the meeting, the die is cast. You cannot complain afterwards. You have to make your objections known in the meeting. For example, make sure the assessor doesn't ask you to include in your system things that do not exist in the Standard.

And as we have seen in Chapter 10, there are many clauses in the Standard that are not obligatory. Some parts of the Standard may simply not apply to you.

If the assessor refuses to give way, you can appeal to the certification body.

Win or lose?

Assuming the assessor finds no major non-conformances, the certification body will send you a certificate. This is the cause of much celebration in most companies.

Don't be disheartened if the assessor fails you. Most of the system is probably in place and you will simply need to correct the few errors the assessor has pointed out.

The certification body will take money off you for every visit it makes. That is how it gets its income. So it will be pleased to offer you a date for another assessment.

Reward your staff

When you get ISO 9000 (BS 5750), it will be because of your staff's effort. So demonstrate your appreciation. Have a party, hand out a commemorative gift, and thank key staff for their input.

This could be a good time to remind staff of the real meaning of ISO 9000 – it's a tool to help your organisation be more effective. It should improve your competitiveness, and safeguard their jobs. But the system has to be maintained. They should actively contribute by corrective action, by audits, and by avoiding short-cuts at the expense of record keeping.

WHY DO THEY DO IT?

25,000 companies in the UK have ISO 9000. What were their reasons for getting it? And what kinds of companies go for it? Research shows that over half the companies are seeking ISO 9000 to satisfy their customers. The other main reason (21 per cent) is the desire to improve efficiency.

ISO 9000 is most popular among engineering firms (43 per cent of the total). This is followed by other manufacturers (17 per cent) and distribution/hotels. Other service businesses were still few in number (1 per cent).

THE BENEFITS TO YOUR BUSINESS

Why do you want to go for ISO 9000? What benefits are you looking for? Put the answers in Table 13.1 below, and try to be specific. Identifying your goals will help you gain the advantages you are looking for. You could use the answers to frame your project's objectives. For example, one objective might be to use ISO 9000 to launch an export drive.

Table 13.1 The reasons we want ISO 9000

What do we expect to get from ISO 9000?

THE REASONS WHY COMPANIES FAIL

When a company fails in its attempt to get ISO 9000, it is usually for a predictable and common reason. Here are the more usual ones.

■ The manual doesn't cover all the requirements of the standard.
■ Staff don't follow the set procedures.
■ Records are not kept.
■ Different versions of the same document are in circulation.
■ The company has not audited the system.
■ The company does not have a clear organisation structure.
■ There are no procedures for important parts of the process.
■ Orders are not reviewed before being processed.
■ Design briefs are not provided.
■ The designs are not verified or checked against the brief. This applies only to ISO 9001 (BS 5750 Part 1).
■ Products cannot be traced. It is not possible to tell whether products have passed or failed inspection.
■ Inspections are not carried out at the proper places (for example, when raw materials arrive).
■ Measuring equipment is not calibrated.
■ Products are not stored properly.

The underlying causes

Behind these failings are some common and deeper problems. They are as follows:

■ Top management is not committed to getting ISO 9000.
■ The company only wants ISO 9000 for the sake of getting the certificate.
■ The company has not spent enough time implementing the standard before applying for certification.
■ The quality manager has not been able to convince line managers of the value of ISO 9000.
■ The quality manager is expected to do too many other jobs.

If these are the kind of problems facing your organisation, you need to take steps to improve matters before the assessors arrive.

SUMMARY

■ Ask more than one certification body for a quotation.
■ When you have chosen a certification body, it will check your manual to see if it complies with ISO 9000.
■ If your manual passes the test, the certification body will visit your site. An assessor will see if the procedures in your manual are being followed.
■ The assessor will work his way through your departments, looking for gaps in the system. If he finds any major 'non-conformances', he may refuse to award you a certificate.
■ Don't accept the assessor's views unquestioningly. Assessors have been known to be wrong.
■ Reward your staff when you get ISO 9000.
■ The majority of companies get ISO 9000 to satisfy their customers' requirements. The number of manufacturers with ISO 9000 still greatly outweighs the number of service companies.
■ Companies fail to get ISO 9000 for a number of reasons. They include: an inadequate manual, procedures not carried out, and records not kept.
■ When a company fails to get ISO 9000, it may be because top management was not committed, not enough time was allowed, or the quality manager was asked to do too many other jobs.

14

BUILDING ON YOUR SYSTEM

◆

In this chapter, you'll learn about:

■ Surveillance visits.
■ How to promote your success.
■ Building on ISO 9000.

SURVEILLANCE VISITS

To make sure you are keeping your system in operation, the certification body will visit your plant every six months for a short check. This is called a surveillance visit.

The surveillance visits will be unannounced. You may get a day or two's notice, but you should work on the assumption that they will turn up tomorrow.

The assessor will look to see if paperwork is up to date. Staff have a habit of letting it slip, and then doing it all in one go. Failure to check something until the end of the week could mean that something has gone wrong for a whole week before it gets noticed.

Your certificate will be valid for three years. At the end of the three years, the certification body may do a complete re-assessment of your site. This is likely to be shorter than your initial assessment, but more extensive than the surveillance visits. Your certificate is then renewed for a further three years.

Your internal audits should therefore check that paperwork is done routinely. If staff are constantly failing, perhaps you need to simplify the paperwork. Ask yourself what happens to the paperwork. Ask yourself what value it provides. What action do people take as a result of it? If the paperwork doesn't tell you anything, you should consider abolishing it.

HOW TO PROMOTE YOUR SUCCESS

ISO 9000 not only improves the way you work, but it gives you an edge over your competitors. So don't be shy – go and tell the world that you've got it. Here we consider some of the ways you can do that.

A press announcement

Start with a press release. Tell your trade press and local press that you've won ISO 9000. Get someone famous to present you with the award. Get the most out of the opportunity – it's an occasion you can never repeat. Make sure your marketing department is organised well in advance.

Be prepared for a lack of coverage. The media has seen and reported these events for many years. So you'll have to try a little harder. Maybe you could have your certificate delivered in an unusual and photogenic way, whether by balloon or by a quality car like a vintage Rolls Royce.

You can ensure press coverage by asking a local newspaper or magazine to do an 'advertorial', or paid editorial feature. The publication gives you editorial coverage in proportion to the amount of advertising it manages to squeeze out of your suppliers. This results in advertisements which say, for example, 'Congratulations on getting ISO 9000, from Smith Ltd, suppliers of janitorial materials'.

Tell your customers

Most importantly, you need to tell your customers. The ordinary consumer doesn't really understand ISO 9000. So until the symbol becomes better known, there may not be much point in telling them. The trade, however, is a different matter. In many industries, acquiring ISO 9000 gets you on to tender lists and preferred supplier lists.

Start with your key accounts, or your most important customers. Consider holding a celebratory event. This will promote the fact that you have got ISO 9000, and it will be a good excuse to get close to your big customers. Bear in mind that the event will have to be well organised. People will take great pleasure in pointing out any faults in your administration if you promote yourself as a quality business.

Ensure that all your other customers know that you have gained ISO 9000. Do this by direct mail or a newsletter.

Make sure they know what advantages your ISO 9000 gives them. Will they have noticed a gradual improvement as you moved towards registration? Can you point to a reduction in complaints? Are you producing fewer faulty products? Try and quantify the changes that will benefit the customer.

Get listed

Check, too, that your firm has been entered in the certification body's

Directory of Approved Suppliers. Other certified companies may use this directory to choose suppliers. The directory may help them choose you.

You can also use the Directory the other way – look in the directory for companies which might need your goods, and then contact them. Tell them that you, too, are registered to ISO 9000 by the same certification body.

Promote your rejects

A marketing director regularly takes potential customers around the plant. He walks them to a cordoned-off area, marked 'Rejects', and proudly points out the rejected material. 'Prior to ISO 9000, it might have gone to customers,' he says. The customers peer at the material. 'I can't see any faults,' they say. 'Neither can I,' says the Marketing Director, triumphantly. 'It just shows you how high our standards are, and what excellent products you'll receive.'

Where you can and can't use the ISO symbol

You can put the ISO 9000 symbol on your letterhead, but not on your products. You can also put it on your vehicles. This gives haulage companies something of an unfair advantage, since their lorries are also their products.

BUILDING ON ISO 9000

ISO 9000 is a big hurdle. It might be the biggest achievement in your company's history. And you can rightfully pat yourself on the back when you get it. You can afford to rest on your laurels – for just a little while.

But in time you could look for another challenge. There are several choices, and knowing what they are will be useful in helping you plan the future.

Refresh your system

Your system will go from novelty to maturity. Once you have had it for two or three years, it will be time to re-examine it. Are some procedures unnecessary? Can you simplify the system or make it easier to understand?

Extend the system to other departments

In Chapter 5, we looked at extending the system to incorporate other departments or subsidiaries. There are merits in having the whole business working on one system. For example, it improves the information flow to the centre.

Go for TQM (Total Quality Management)

Many organisations use ISO 9000 as the starting point for a comprehensive attack on quality failings. TQM seeks to change the attitudes of the workforce, by encouraging them to understand the needs of customers, both internal and external.

Introduce other quality programmes

If quality of service is important for your organisation, you might consider introducing a customer care programme. Or you might introduce statistical process control. By the time you get ISO 9000 certification, you'll know what's best for you.

Get certified to BS 7750

BS 7750 helps you manage the environment, in the same way that ISO 9000 helps you manage quality. BS 7750 is based on ISO 9000. For example, both use the principles of document control and internal audits. So companies with the quality standard are already a long way towards getting the environment standard.

Many people believe that corporate customers will soon expect their suppliers to be registered to BS 7750, just as they now expect them to have ISO 9000.

Case history: How ISO 9000 saved a major contract

ISO 9000 saved one company's biggest contract. The company in question supplies parts to car manufacturers like Jaguar and Land Rover.

'At one time we had pallet-loads of returns from Ford, our biggest customer,' says the company's quality manager. 'Now we only get the odd unit back in a month. We get so few returns, they're hardly worth bothering with. ISO 9000 has made the difference.'

The standard, he reckons is very flexible. It tells you what it wants to see, and lets you design the system. As long as you document what you do, the assessors are happy.

When he introduced ISO 9000, its newness was a problem to the workforce. They were uncertain what it meant for them, he says. They thought it would clutter them up with more and more paperwork. 'Another bright idea', they would say.

The quality manager ran half-day seminars for the work force, and this helped to change attitudes (though as he points out, you always get cynics).

He also uses ISO 9000 to get management involvement. 'I got the sales manager and the managing director to be internal auditors,' he says. 'They find out what's happening in the company. They're also a fresh pair of eyes, so they pick up things I miss. It also means that the works see management commitment to quality.'

The effects on the company's profits is hard to calculate, but the quality manager reckons that there are real advantages. 'We're not wasting people's time any more,' he says. 'Things are in the right place. The place is better managed. And people's attitudes have changed for the good.

'We're also looking to expand into new markets, he says. And having ISO 9000 helped us win a big new contract.'

Customers and suppliers

The company is finding that its customers use ISO 9000 to choose their suppliers. The quality manager says, 'We find that, more and more, government purchasing agencies are saying to us, "If you want to tender, you need ISO 9000. If you haven't got it, don't bother tendering".

'All of the automotive industry uses ISO 9000. That includes Ford and Rolls Royce, whose standards are substantially based on ISO 9000. If you have ISO 9000, you can skip the first part of Ford's three-part assessment.'

In turn, the quality manager is putting pressure on *his* suppliers. 'We're telling our suppliers that they should have ISO 9000. It's the only way I can have confidence in my supplier base. We've written off numerous longstanding suppliers – that's what happens if they won't come to the party.'

SUMMARY

■   After giving you an ISO 9000 certificate, the certification body will make a surveillance visit twice a year. This is to make sure you maintain the system.

■   After getting your certificate, you should publicise your success. You can issue a press release, or have an award ceremony. You should tell your customers.

- You should also tell companies who do not presently buy from you. Your new status as an ISO 9000 business may make them change their minds.
- Check carefully where you use the ISO 9000 logo. For example, you can't put it on your packaging.
- Once the dust has settled, consider building on your system. You might go for TQM. Or you might decide to improve your ISO 9000 system. Alternatively, you might go for BS 7750, the environmental standard.

APPENDIX 1

◆

The Standard translated into plain English

This translation reveals the main idea in each clause of the standard.

To make it easier to grasp the sense, the translation omits some of the trailing clauses and qualifications which clutter the standard.

Where there is a choice between clarity and word-for-word imitation, the translation opts for clarity.

Once you have understood the general intent of each clause, you should check with the Standard itself, to see if there are any details which might affect you.

You shouldn't base your system on the translation, because it is a simplification. But it should help you understand the meaning of the Standard.

The headings of the Standard are just as unfriendly as the clauses themselves. So they, too, have been translated. The standard starts at clause four, the first three clauses being introductory comments.

Comparing Part 1 and Part 2

This is a translation of ISO 9001 (BS 5750 Part 1). There is a simpler standard called ISO 9002 (BS 5750 Part 2) which omits clause 4.4 (Design control). We discuss the difference in Chapter 5.

4 WHAT THE SYSTEM REQUIRES

4.1 Management's responsibilities

4.1.1 Quality policy

The Board member responsible for quality should produce a policy document that shows your company's commitment to quality.

This policy must be understood and implemented at all levels in your organisation.

4.1.2 Organisation

4.1.2.1 Responsibility and authority

You should identify the people whose work affects quality. State in writing their responsibilities and relationships.

You should include those who have to:

- Take action to prevent problems with the product.
- Notice and record quality problems.
- Recommend solutions.
- Check that the solutions have been carried out.
- Manage the unsatisfactory product or process until it has been rectified.

4.1.2.2 Resources

You should assess what resources you need to maintain your quality. Make sure they are adequate. Assign trained people to do the work.

4.1.2.3 Management representative

The Board member responsible for quality should appoint a manager to be responsible for the quality system. He should:

a) Implement and maintain the quality system.

b) Report on the quality system to senior management.

4.1.3 Management review

The Board member responsible for quality should have a regular meeting to review any problems concerning the system. Keep a record of each meeting.

4.2 Quality system

4.2.1 General

The Board member responsible for quality should have a system that ensures your product is produced the way you planned. You should have a manual which explains how your system works.

4.2.2 Procedures

a) You must have written instructions stating how work shall be carried out.

b) You must also ensure that the instructions are carried out in practice.

4.2.3 Quality planning

You should write down how your quality needs will be met. You should consider doing the following:

a) Have quality plans.

b) Have controls, processes and skills for achieving the right quality.

c) Ensure that all elements of the work process are compatible.

d) Update quality control and testing techniques.

e) Develop capability in taking measurements.

f) Identify what checks need to be made.

g) Identify acceptable work standards.

h) Keep quality records.

4.3 Order checking

4.3.1 General

You should have written procedures for checking your contracts or orders before you fulfil them.

4.3.2 Review

You should review each contract or order to check that:

a) The customer has specified what he wants.

b) You have resolved any differences between the tender and the order.

c) You can actually fulfil the order.

4.3.3 Amendments to orders

You should identify how changes are made to orders. Changes must be correctly transmitted to your relevant departments.

4.3.4 Records

Keep a record of the checks you make on orders received.

4.4 Design control (Does not apply to ISO 9002)

4.4.1 General

You should have procedures to check that the design of your product is done the way you intended it to be.

4.4.2 Design planning

You should plan each design activity. This includes allocating people's responsibilities. You should have a written procedure for this.

You should allocate the design work to qualified people. You should give them adequate resources.

4.4.3 Communicating with other departments

Decide how people in different departments and different technologies should work together. Make sure you tell them in writing, and review your plans often.

4.4.⸗ The design brief

Decide what information your design department needs to create a design. Include any legal requirements. Ensure that the department gets written briefs. Carry out regular checks to make sure the information is still adequate.

Ensure that the design department resolves any incomplete, ambiguous or conflicting briefs with the person who drew up the brief.

Include in the brief the results of any order checking.

4.4.5 Design review

You should hold design review meetings at appropriate stages. Include staff from all relevant departments. Keep minutes of the meetings.

4.4.6 The resulting design

The designers should state how the design performs, to demonstrate that it meets the brief.

a) The design must meet the brief.

b) The designers must show that the design meets the acceptance criteria from the brief.

c) The designers must show how the product can be safely operated.

d) The designers must review the product's documents before it is released.

4.4.7 Checking that the design is right

You should check that the design meets the brief. You should record what checks are to be made.

Apart from holding design reviews, you can also:

a) Do alternative calculations.

b) Compare the design with a similar proven design.

c) Test the new design.

d) Review the design documents.

4.4.8 Design validation

You should check that the product meets the customer's needs, as specified in the order.

4.4.9 Changing the design

You should write down the design changes you make. Ensure that changes are approved by authorised people.

4.5 Controlling important documents

4.5.1 General

You should have a written method for controlling the documents that relate to your quality system. This includes external documents, such as customer drawings.

4.5.2 Approving and issuing documents

The documents should be checked by the right people before being issued.

You should keep a master list of the current documents. This will prevent people from using out-of-date copies.

a) You should ensure that up-to-date copies of the documents are available whenever they are needed.

b) Out-of-date documents must be promptly removed from use.

c) You must identify any archived documents which you are keeping for legal reasons.

4.5.3 Modifying and changing documents

Changes to documents should be checked by the same people who checked the original ones. These people should have background information to help them make the right decision when checking the changes.

Where possible, you should identify the nature of the change in the document.

4.6 Purchasing

4.6.1 General

You should make sure that your purchases do what you require of them.

4.6.2 Evaluating your suppliers

a) You should choose suppliers according to whether they can meet your needs. That includes achieving the right quality.

b) You should define how you will control your suppliers. This will depend on the item bought, its impact on the quality of your final product, and the supplier's previous performance.

c) You should keep records of acceptable suppliers.

4.6.3 Purchasing data

Your purchase orders should clearly describe what you are ordering. This could include:

a) The type or class of product.

b) A reference to a specific drawing or other technical data.

c) The relevant international standard.

You should check and approve purchase orders before issuing them.

4.6.4 Checking purchases

4.6.4.1 Verifying your supplier's product

If you want to check your purchases at a supplier's premises, you should specify this in your purchase order.

4.6.4.2 *Your customer's checks*

If the contract requires it, you should let your customer check that he is going to get what he ordered. These checks could be at your premises or those of your supplier. You should not take his check as proof of your supplier's quality.

The check doesn't free you from the responsibility of providing acceptable products. And your customer can reject the goods later, if need be.

4.7 Looking after products that belong to your customer

Decide how to look after any product belonging to your customer that is in your care. Put this in writing. Make sure you tell your customer if you damage or lose anything that belongs to him.

4.8 Identifying and tracing your products

Where appropriate, you should be able to identify your product at all stages of production and afterwards.

If you need to trace your product, each product or batch should be specially marked. Make sure you keep proper records.

4.9 Controlling your production process

You should properly plan your production process. You should ensure that production is carried out under controlled conditions. This includes the installation and servicing of your product.

a) You should have written procedures. They should tell your staff how to produce, install and service your product. Do this in cases where the absence of written information would affect quality.

b) You should use suitable production equipment, and have a suitable work environment.

c) You should comply with relevant standards, quality plans or written instructions.

d) You should monitor and control important aspects of the production process. This includes the installation and servicing of your product.

e) You should control how processes and equipment are approved.

f) You should state what level of workmanship you expect. Do this by having written standards or sample materials.

g) You should maintain your equipment properly.

Processes that can't be checked (special processes)

The effectiveness of some processes cannot be checked once they are completed. In such cases a defect will only be revealed when the product is being used.

To ensure that such products are free of faults, the process should be carried out by qualified operators. You may also need to provide continuous monitoring and control the process.

You should specify what kind of equipment and staff training is needed.

You will also need to keep proper records about the process, the equipment and staff.

4.10 Inspection and test

4.10.1 General

You should have written instructions for inspecting your product. You should specify what records should be kept.

4.10.2 Checks at goods inwards

4.10.2.1 Incoming materials should not be used until you have checked that they meet your stated requirements. You should write down the testing methods and the records to be kept.

4.10.2.2 In deciding how to check incoming goods, you should take into account the quality of your supplier, and any written evidence of quality that he provides.

4.10.2.3 You may have to release incoming materials because production staff need them urgently. If this happens, you should positively identify them, so that you can recall them if they are later found to be faulty.

4.10.3 Checks during your process

a) You should check the product as required by your written procedures or quality plan.

b) Don't allow your product to go forward until you have done all the tests, or received the right reports.

One exception to this is where you release the product having first marked it, so that you can recall it if you later discover it was faulty. When this happens, you should still make sure that all the proper tests are done.

4.10.4 Final checks

You should carry out final inspection as stated in your written procedures.

Your procedures should require the product to have passed all inspections. This includes receiving inspection and in-process checks.

You should not send out a product until all the action specified in your written procedures has been carried out. Nor should you send out a product until you have received and approved the relevant documents.

4.10.5 Keeping records of your checks

You should keep inspection records. They should show whether the product passed or failed. If the product failed, you should take the action described in 4.13 below (Control of faulty products).

Your records should show who approved the product.

4.11 The equipment you use for checking

4.11.1 General

You should write down how you will control and maintain any equipment which is used to check that the product is of the right quality.

You should know how accurate your equipment is. The equipment should be capable of making the required measurements.

Any software used to test your product must be checked prior to its release. You should re-check it at intervals. You should decide the scale and frequency of the checks, and keep records of them.

If necessary, let your customer see what checks you carry out. This will let him satisfy himself that the checks are adequate.

4.11.2 Controlling your inspection equipment

a) You should decide what goods are to be measured, and how accurate the measurements should be. You should choose the right equipment for the job.

b) You should check your equipment against a national standard. If no national standard exists, you should state in writing how you will check the equipment.

c) You should specify in writing how checks will be carried out. You will need to identify the equipment, its reference number and location.

You will also need to specify how often the checks should be made, the method of checking, and what to do if the machine is found to be inaccurate.

d) Mark the measuring equipment or keep a record to show whether it has been approved for use in calibration.

e) Keep records of your checks.

f) If the equipment is found to be inaccurate, you should check the validity of previous test results. You should note your findings in writing.

g) Ensure that environmental conditions allow measurements to be carried out effectively.

h) Make sure that the equipment is handled and stored carefully so that it stays accurate.

i) Don't let people adjust the test equipment and software. This might affect its accuracy.

4.12 Identifying whether your goods have passed inspection

You should be able to show which products have been inspected and approved.

You should continue to identify whether products have passed or failed inspection throughout the production and installation of a product. This will ensure that customers receive only products which have passed the tests.

You should define in writing how the product's inspection status will be made evident.

4.13 Control of faulty products

4.13.1 General

You should have written systems for preventing faulty products from getting to the customer. These systems must be maintained.

Your controls should identify any faulty product, check it, and segregate it (where practical). You should record it in writing, dispose of it properly, and notify relevant people.

4.13.2 What to do about faulty products

You should define who is responsible for deciding what to do with faulty products.

There are four things you can do about faulty products. They are:

a) You can re-work it to the right quality.

b) You can accept it (with or without repair).

c) You can regrade it for a different use.

d) You can reject or scrap it.

If your customer's contract requires you to report the faulty product to him for possible acceptance, you should see if he wishes to accept it. You should record the fault that has been accepted, and any repairs you have made.

After repairing or re-working a product, you should re-inspect it according to your normal procedures.

4.14 Taking action to cure and prevent faults

4.14.1 General

You should have a written method for curing and preventing faults. Any action should reflect the scale of the problem and the risk.

When you take action to prevent or cure problems, you should change your written procedures.

4.14.2 Correcting faults

You should have a written method for curing faults. Include the following:

a) Deal effectively with customer complaints and reports of product faults.

b) Investigate the causes of any product or process faults, and record your findings.

c) Decide what action you need to take to eliminate the cause of the fault.

d) Apply controls to make sure that corrective actions are taken, and that they work.

4.14.3 Preventing faults

You should have a written method for preventing faults. Include the following:

a) Use information (such as audit results) to eliminate potential problems.

b) Decide how to deal with problems that require preventative action.

c) Take preventative action; apply controls to make sure it works.

d) When you take action, tell your management review meeting.

4.15 Handling, storage, packaging, preservation and delivery

4.15.1 General

You should decide the best way to handle, store, package, preserve and deliver your product. Put this in writing, and make sure staff adopt this method.

4.15.2 Handling

Make sure your product is handled in a way that prevents damage or deterioration.

4.15.3 Storage

You should have storage areas or a stock room which protects the products from damage or deterioration, before they are used or delivered.

You should state how products will be taken in and out of storage. You should check the stock for deterioration at suitable intervals.

4.15.4 Packaging

Ensure that your packaging and labelling maintains the quality of the product.

4.15.5 Preservation

You must preserve and segregate the product for as long as you are responsible for it.

4.15.6 Delivery

You should protect the quality of the product after its final inspection. If you are responsible for delivery, you should ensure that the delivery method protects the quality of the product.

4.16 Quality records

You should decide the best way of keeping records. You need to decide how to identify, index, store and dispose of them.

Your quality records should demonstrate that your products are of the required quality. The records should also show that your quality system is working properly.

You should also keep records of your suppliers.

The records should be legible, and you should be able to retrieve them easily. You should store them in an environment which minimises deterioration or damage.

You should state in writing how long records will be kept.

Where you have agreed it with your customer, you should let him inspect your records for an agreed period.

Note: You can keep the records on your computer.

4.17 Internal quality audits

You should carry out audits on your quality system. The audits should check whether staff are following the written procedures. They should also check that your quality system is effective.

The audits should be planned, and put in writing. The amount of time spent auditing each area will depend on how important it is.

Audits shall be carried out by staff who are independent of those whose work is being examined.

Put the findings of the audits in writing. Give a copy to the people responsible for the area that has been audited. Make sure they correct any problems revealed in the audit.

Follow-up audits should check whether effective corrective action has been taken.

4.18 Training

Decide what training is needed for everyone whose job affects the quality of your product. Put it in writing, and make sure it happens.

You should only give people jobs for which they are qualified by education, training and experience.

Keep adequate records of training.

4.19 Servicing

If you are contracted to service your product, you should write down how servicing will be carried out. Make sure this happens in practice.

4.20 Using statistics

4.20.1 Identifying the need for statistics

You should see whether you need statistics to assess and control the quality of your process and product.

4.20.2 Procedures

If you identify any suitable statistics in 4.20.1 above, you should put in writing how they should be collected. Make sure this happens in practice.

APPENDIX 2

◆

Jargon beater

What do people mean when they talk about 'Part 2'? What are the differences between certification, registration and accreditation? And where does verification fit in?

Here is a simple explanation of what the jargon means. It avoids the laborious definitions such as you see at the beginning of an international standard.

Accreditation body An official organisation appointed to check that *certification* bodies are competent to award certificates. The accreditation body is appointed by a national government or similar national body. In the UK, the accreditation body is the NACCB (National Accreditation Council for Certification Bodies).

Assessment An *audit* of your whole system by a *certification* body.

Assessor An auditor who checks the whole of a quality assurance system. Usually works for a *certification body*.

Audit A check that the quality system is operating as it should. An audit can be a desk exercise (to check your manual conforms to ISO 9000). But it more commonly involves visiting a site or department to see whether it is conforming to written procedures.

BS 5750 A standard for quality systems. The same as ISO 9000. You can get certified to Part 1, which is for design and production; or to Part 2, which is for production only.

Calibrate, to To check the accuracy of measuring equipment.

Certificate A piece of paper you proudly display in your reception, proving that you have a quality assurance system that has been approved by an independent organisation.

Certification Once you install a quality system, you can apply to have it independently checked (or certified) by a certification body. If the certification body approves your system, it will give you a certificate.

Certification body A certification body assesses your quality system to see if it conforms to the standard.

Conformance Doing it right.

Controlled document A document which is formally issued to a particular department or job title. This document must be kept up to date, by means of revisions controlled by the *quality manager*.

Document, to To put something in writing. The Standard expects you to document anything that might affect your quality.

Document control Document control has a precise meaning in the Standard. It means ensuring that only current copies of key documents (for example *work instructions*) are allowed to be in circulation. It means having a system for recalling out-of-date documents, and issuing new ones in their place. It means specifying who should get copies of these *controlled documents*.

EN 29000 Exactly the same standard as BS 5750. This name is used by European companies and the EC.

Final inspection The last check on a product before it is sent to a customer. Your last chance to get it right!

First party audit An *internal audit* of your own quality system, carried out by your own staff.

Implementation Installing a quality system in your organisation.

Internal audit A check which is carried out by your staff on all or part of your quality system. It is the same as a *first party audit*.

ISO 9000 Exactly the same standard as BS 5750. The term ISO 9000 is more common outside the UK and Europe. ISO 9001 is the same as BS 5750 Part 1, while ISO 9002 is the same as BS 5750 Part 2.

Maintain ISO 9000 expects you to keep the system working. That is why staff must 'own' the system and believe in it. An external assessor will check twice a year to see that you are maintaining the system.

Management Review   A regular meeting held with senior management to check the effectiveness of the quality system.

Materiel   Not a spelling error, materiel is a collective noun that covers equipment and supplies. It is a rather old fashioned quality term that came from the military.

Non-conformance   A fault or error of some kind. Specifically, it means that part of the system is not working the way you planned it. The term 'non-conformity' means the same thing.

Owning the system   Your staff will only accept ISO 9000 if they have had a part in developing it.

Part 1, Part 2   Abbreviation for BS 5750: Part 1 and Part 2. If you opt for Part 1, the *assessment* will cover your production and design departments. Part 2 includes only your production.

Procedure   A method of doing a particular type of job. In ISO 9000 this is written down. If everyone knows what the right procedure is, fewer errors will be made.

Product   In ISO 9000, the 'product' is whatever you produce, whether it be tractors or insurance policies. It refers equally to services.

Purchaser   In the language of the Standard, this means your customer.

Quality   For ISO 9000, quality means 'fit for the purpose'. That implies you are providing a product or service which meets your customer's need.

Quality assurance   A term to denote a system which aims to ensure that quality is in-built, by means of written *procedures* and good communication.

Quality control   Implies the control of quality by means of inspection. It is a means of picking faulty goods from among perfect goods. An old fashioned approach compared with *quality assurance*.

Quality manager   The person who oversees the quality system.

Quality manual Usually a set of ring binders which contain all the procedures and forms required by ISO 9000.

Quality plan A document setting out the way you ensure the quality of a particular product or project. This is often done by companies constructing a new building or an oil pipeline. It contrasts with a quality system because it usually deals with a one-off contract.

Quality policy A brief statement, often signed by the Chief Executive, outlining the company's commitment towards quality.

Quality system A quality system consists of procedures, responsibilities, organisation structure and resources working together to meet specific quality requirements. ISO 9000 gives you a structured quality system.

Registration Another word for *certification*. It means being registered with a *certification body*.

Second party audit An audit by an organisation which has a commercial interest, such as a major customer who visits your site.

Sub-contractor Your supplier. The term comes from the military. They saw themselves as the main contractor, when they owned shipyards which built warships. So any company from whom they bought parts was a 'sub-contractor'.

Supplier In the language of the Standard, this means you, assuming you are installing a quality system in your organisation. This book avoids using the term in this sense, because it is confusing.

Third party audit An *audit* by an independent *certification* body. When you are assessed for ISO 9000 certification, you undergo a third party audit.

Traceability The ability to check a product back through a production process. Traceability tells you who made what, or who did it when. Traceability is important if you need to recall a product, or trace a fault.

Vendor A potential supplier.

Verify, to To check that something is right. This can include inspection, testing and auditing.

Verification Checking.

Work instruction   A detailed *procedure*. Explains the step-by-step action required to do a job.

APPENDIX 3

◆

Where to get help

There is a lot of useful information about ISO 9000. It is worth collecting some of this material, to get ideas and to see whether the organisations listed below can help you.

Collect the free information first, before deciding whether to pay for training or consultancy. Start with the unbiased sources of information (such as government bodies) before moving on to the more commercial organisations who want to sell you something. But bear in mind that most of the organisations will have their own agenda, which may not coincide with your needs.

The government

Department of Trade and Industry
In Britain, the DTI publishes useful free booklets on ISO 9000 and related subjects.

The DTI will also give unbiased advice to businesses. It may refer you to its local office, which will have an even better understanding of local needs and facilities.

In the past, the DTI has offered grants. Find out what assistance you might get. See if it is providing money to help companies get ISO 9000. See what other services it offers, such as organising visits to companies which have ISO 9000.

Department of Trade and Industry
151 Buckingham Palace Road
London SW1W 9SS
Tel: 0800 500 200 (free)

Many DTI publications and videos are available from:

Mediascene Ltd
PO Box 90
Hengoed
Mid Glamorgan CF8 9YE
Tel: (0443) 821877
Fax: (0443) 822055

You can also talk to your regional office. You can get its address and telephone number from the London office (above).

Training and Enterprise Councils (TECs)

In the UK, TECs are government agencies which provide training and advice to business, especially small companies. There are over 80 TECs in England and Wales, and over 20 in Scotland (where they are called Local Enterprise Companies or LECs).

TECs are a good source of advice and information on ISO 9000. They may also provide a grant, or tell you where you can get one.

Practice varies from one TEC to another. If you are lucky enough to have a local TEC which believes quality is important, you could receive a lot of help.

You may find that your local TEC provides mainly evening training, and on a group basis. You may also find that it lacks experience of your industry. But it is worth investigating for its low cost and impartiality.

Employment Department
Management and Trainer Development
Room E603, Moorfoot, Sheffield S1 4PQ.

In Scotland, contact: Scottish Enterprise National, 120 Bothwell St, Glasgow G2 7JP.

Quality bodies

National Accreditation Council for Certification Bodies (NACCB)
This is an impartial organisation that checks certification bodies. It publishes a list of all approved certification bodies, including the scope of their activities. There is a charge for this list.

The Secretary
NACCB
Audley House
13 Palace St
London SW1E 5HS
Tel: 071-233 7111
Fax: 071-233 5115

The British Standards Institution
This organisation publishes British standards. It may also have information and publications about quality assurance and standards.

A copy of ISO 9001 or 9002 is essential if you intend to get certified. You can order copies direct from BSI, from HMSO, and certain bookshops. You can also find copies of British Standards in bigger libraries.

Communications Department
BSI
Linford Wood
Milton Keynes MK14 6LE
Tel: (0908) 220022

Certification

Association of British Certification bodies (ABCB)
The ABCB is the national organisation for certification bodies. Its members independently verify that your quality system conforms to ISO 9000. You can ask them for a list of members.

The Committee Administrator
ABCB
2 Park St
London W1A 2BS
Tel: 071-495 4193
Fax: 071-495 4190

In the UK, the biggest certification body is BSI QA, which is owned by BSI. There are over 20 other certification bodies. Most have brochures; a few also have useful free booklets. Some may have specialised information relating to your industry. The following have been accredited by NACCB (see above).

Associated Offices Quality Certification Ltd, Longridge House, Longridge Place, Manchester M60 4DT. Tel: 061-833 2295.

ASTA Certification Services, Prudential Chambers, 23 Market Place, Rugby CV21 3DU. Tel: (0788) 578435.

BMT Quality Assessors Ltd, Scottish Metropolitan Alpha Centre, Stirling University Innovation Park, Stirling FK9 4NF. Tel: (0786) 50891.

BSI QA, PO Box 375, Milton Keynes MK14 6LL. Tel: (0908) 220908.

British Approvals Service for Electrical Cables, Silbury Court, 360 Silbury Boulevard, Milton Keynes MK9 2AF. Tel: (0908) 691121.

Bureau Veritas Quality International, 70 Borough High St, London SE1 1XF. Tel: 071-378 8113.

Central Certification Service Ltd, Victoria House, 123 Midland Road, Wellingborough, Northants NN8 1LU. Tel: (0933) 441796.

Ceramic Industry Certification Scheme Ltd, Queens Road, Penkhull, Stoke on Trent, ST4 7LQ. Tel: (0782) 411008.

Construction Quality Assurance, Arcade Chambers, The Arcade, Market Place, Newark NG24 1UD. Tel: (0636) 708700.

Det Norske Veritas QA, Veritas House, 112 Station Road, Sidcup DA15 7BU. Tel: 081-309 7477.

Electrical Association Quality Assurance Ltd, 30 Millbank, London SW1P 4RD. Tel: 071-828 9227.

Electrical Equipment Certification Service, Health and Safety Executive, Harpur Hill, Buxton, Derbyshire SK17 9JN. Tel: (0298) 26211.

Engineering Inspection Authorities Board, IME, 1 Birdcage Walk, London SW1H 9JJ. Tel: 071-973 1271.

Lloyds Register QA, Norfolk House, Wellesley Road, Croydon CR9 2DT. Tel: 081-688 6882.

National Approval Council for Security Systems, Queensgate House, 14 Cookham Rd, Maidenhead SL6 8AJ. Tel: (0628) 37512.

National Inspection Council Quality Assurance, 5 Cotswold Business Park, Millfield Lane, Caddington LU1 4AR. Tel: (0582) 841144.

SIRA Certification Service, Saighton Lane, Saighton, Chester CH3 6EG. Tel: (0244) 332200.

The Loss Prevention Certification Board, Melrose Ave, Borehamwood, Herts WD6 2BJ. Tel: 081-207 2345.

The Quality Scheme for Ready Mixed Concrete, 3 High St, Hampton, Middlesex TW12 2SQ. Tel: 081-941 0273.

Trada Quality Assurance Services Ltd, Stocking Lane, Hughenden Valley, High Wycombe, Bucks HP14 4NR. Tel: (0240) 245484.

UK Certificating Authority for Reinforcing Steels, Oak House, Tubs Hill, Sevenoaks, Kent TN13 1BL. Tel: (0732) 450000.

SGS Yarsley, Trowers Way, Redhill, Surrey RH1 2JN. Tel: (0737) 768445.

Steel Construction QA Scheme Ltd, 4 Whitehall Court, London SW1A 2ES. Tel: 071-839 8566.

Water Industry Certification Scheme, Frankland Rd, Blagrove, Swindon SN5 8YF. Tel: (0793) 410005.

Quality bodies

Institute of Quality Assurance (IQA)

The IQA is a professional body for those involved with quality assurance. It organises seminars and conferences on all aspect of quality. It also administers a formal training course.

IQA
10 Grosvenor Gardens
London SW1W 0DQ
Tel: 071-823 5609
Fax: 071-824 8030

National Quality Information Centre (NQIC)

The NQIC is operated by the IQA (above). It aims to help industry and commerce obtain the information and advice they need to improve quality.

NQIC
PO Box 712
61 Southwark St
London SE1 1SB
Tel: 071-401 7227
Fax: 071-401 2725

Quality Methods Association (QMA)

The QMA is a practical user group for companies who want to apply quality methods in their organisations. The QMA provides a forum for the development and exchange of quality practices. It has specialist study groups, training, seminars and an annual conference.

The Administrator
QMA
6a St Mary's Bridge
Plymouth Road
Plympton
Plymouth PL7 4JR
Tel: (0752) 348358
Fax: (0752) 348330

Association of Quality Management Consultants (AQMC)

The AQMC is a self-regulating body whose members are management consultants which specialise in quality.

Honorary Secretary
AQMC
4 Beyne Road
Olivers Battery
Winchester
Hants SO22 4JW
Tel: (0962) 864394
Fax: (0962) 866969

Consultancies

See what information consultancies can offer you. They may have helpful brochures or reprints from magazine articles. There is an Institute of Management Consultancies, to which the bigger consultancies belong. The Department of Trade and Industry may be able to show you where you can get a list of local quality consultancies. There is more information about choosing a consultancy in Chapter 5.

Institute of Management Consultants
32/33 Hatton Garden
London EC1N 8DL
Tel: 071-242 2140
Fax: 071-831 4597

Calibration and testing information

National Measurement Accreditation Service (NAMAS)
If you have equipment that needs calibrating or material that needs testing, you may want a Namas laboratory. This is a measurement laboratory which has been accredited by the National Physical Laboratory (NPL), the UK national standards laboratory. NPL has a Directory of Accredited Laboratories.

Namas Executive
National Physical Laboratory
Teddington
Middlesex TW11 0LW
Tel: 081-943 7140
Fax: 081-943 7134

Your trade association

Ask your trade association if it has any information about ISO 9000. It may have published information about how to apply the Standard in your industry. It may be able to tell you if there is a specialised certification body; and it might put you in touch with companies who have successfully implemented ISO 9000. It might even find you companies which have had a bad experience from ISO 9000. This will help you make up your own mind about the Standard.

Another source of information is your professional body, aimed at individuals in your area of work, such as engineering, accountancy, marketing or computing.

Your chamber of commerce

The chamber of commerce may provide training or talks on ISO 9000. It may be able to give you the names of local consultants. It will also publish a business magazine which carries news about ISO 9000 activities in your area. Ask at your local library, or look in Yellow Pages for the name of your chamber of commerce.

Business magazines

ISO 9000 is a subject likely to be covered in your regional business magazine. Here you will also find companies offering training courses and consultancy. The magazine will also tell you about local seminars and events. You may also find the names of companies who have just been though ISO 9000 and who may be prepared to give you advice.

Trade magazines aimed at your industry may have features on quality, especially if many companies in your sector are applying for it.

Books

Various organisations publish books on ISO 9000 and quality assurance. It is worth seeing whether your library stocks any. If not, the library might order one for you. It is better still to have your own personal copy, because you may need to refer to it over a long period of time.

If you have found this book useful and you now want a book that looks at ISO 9000 in more depth, try *Implementing Quality through BS 5750*, by Jackson and Ashton, published by Kogan Page.

DTI QA Register

The DTI QA Register lists 15,000 companies in the UK and abroad whose quality systems have been assessed to ISO 9000 by a UK certification body. When you get certification, your company should be listed here. You can buy a copy of the Register from HMSO outlets, costing £145.

Guidance Notes

See if there is a set of guidelines for your industry. They exist for industries as varied as banking, the law, food and management consultancy. These guidelines are produced by different organisations, often the trade association or a certification body. The guidelines will show you what ISO 9000 means for your business. They will help you avoid re-inventing the wheel – you will be learning from others' hard work. And remember that the assessor from the certification body will probably have a copy of the guidelines hidden in his briefcase. If you can demonstrate that you understand how ISO 9000 relates to your industry, you get off to a good start.

Take care when using a guidelines document that it doesn't ask to implement a top-heavy system. Make sure that it asks you to do no more than is in the Standard. Some guidelines are based on the experiences of large companies. They may have more staff and a more complex business than you.

The guidelines may have been written by a someone who loves excessive detail or control. Quality people have been known to create whole empires for themselves, by developing large quality systems. Four examples of guidelines are:

Chemicals	Chemical Industries Association
	Kings Buildings
	Smith Square
	London SW1P 3JJ
	Tel: 071-834 3399
	Fax: 071-834 4469
Food Industry	Lloyds Register Quality Assurance Ltd
	Norfolk House
	Wellesley Road
	Croydon CR9 2DT
	Tel: 081-688 6882
	Fax: 081-681 8146
Nursing Homes	BSI QA (address above)
Stockists	BVQI (address above)

International enquiries

You should start by approaching your country's national standards body, many of which are listed below. Remember that this body is responsible for all standards, not just ISO 9000; and the standard may be known by its local title.

Australia
Standards Australia
PO Box 1055
STRATHFIELD – N.S.W. 2135
Tel: +61 2 746 47 00
Fax: +61 2 746 84 50

Austria
Österreichisches
Normungsinstitut
Heinestrasse 38
Postfach 130
A-1021 WIEN
Tel: +43 1 26 75 35
Fax: +43 1 26 75 52

Belgium
Institut belge de normalisation
Av. de la Brabançonne 29
B-1040 BRUXELLES
Tel: +32 2 734 92 05
Fax: +32 2 733 42 64

Brazil
Associação Brasileiro de Normas
Técnicas
Av. 13 de Maio, n° 13, 27° andar
Caixa Postal 1680
CEP: 20003-900 –
RIO DE JANEIRO-RJ
Tel: +55 21 210 31 22
Fax: +55 21 532 21 43

Bulgaria
Committee for Standardization and
Metrology at the Council of Ministers
21, 6th September Str.
1000 SOFIA
Tel: +359 2 85 91
Fax: 359 2 80 14 02

Canada
Standards Council of Canada
45 O'Connor Street, Suite 1200
OTTAWA
ONTARIO
K1P 6N7
Tel: +1 613 238 32 22
Fax: +1 613 995 45 64

China
China State Bureau of Technical
Supervision
4, Zhi Chun Road
Haidian District
P.O. Box 8010
BEIJING 100088
Tel: +86 1 203 24 24
Fax: +86 1 203 10 10

Cyprus
Cyprus Organization for Standards
and Control of Quality
Ministry of Commerce and Industry
NICOSIA
Tel: +357 2 30 34 41
Fax: +357 2 36 61 20

Czech Republic
Czech Office for Standards,
Metrology and Testing
Václavské námestí 19
113 47 PRAHA 1
Tel: +42 2 236 57 34
Fax: +42 2 236 57 06

Denmark
Dansk Standard
Baunegaardsvej 73
DK-2900 HELLERUP
Tel: +45 39 77 01 01
Fax: +45 39 77 02 02

Egypt
Egyptian Organization for
Standardization and Quality Control
2 Latin America Street
Garden City
CAIRO
Tel: +20 2 354 97 20
Fax: +20 2 355 78 41

Finland
Finnish Standards Association SFS
P.O. Box 116
SF-00241 HELSINKI
Tel: +358 0 149 93 31
Fax: +358 0 146 49 25

France
Association française de normalisation
Tour Europe
Cedex 7
F-92049 PARIS LA DÉFENSE
Tel: +331 42 91 55 55
Fax: +331 42 91 56 56

Germany
DIN Deutsches Institut Für Normung
D-10772 BERLIN
Tel: +49 30 26 01-0
Fax: +49 30 26 01 12 31

Greece
Hellenic Organization for
Standardization
313, Acharnon Street
GR-111 45 ATHENS
Tel: +30 1 201 50 25
Fax: +30 1 202 07 76

Hungary
Magyar Szabványügyi Hivatal
1450 BUDAPEST 9
Pf. 24.
Tel: +36 1 218 30 11
Fax: +36 1 218 51 25

India
Bureau of Indian Standards
Manak Bhavan
9 Bahadur Shah Zafar Marg
NEW DELHI 110002
Tel: +91 11 331 79 91
Fax: +91 11 331 40 62

Indonesia
Dewan Standardisasi Nasional – DSN
(Standardization Council of Indonesia)
Pusat Standardisasi-LIPI
Jalan Jend. Gatot Subroto 10
JAKARTA 12710
Tel: +62 21 522 16 86
Fax: +62 21 520 65 74

Ireland
National Standards Authority of
Ireland
Glasnevin
DUBLIN-9
Tel: +353 1 37 01 01
Fax: +353 1 36 98 21

Israel
Standards Institution of Israel
42 Chaim Levanon Street
TEL AVIV 69977
Tel: +972 2 646 51 54
Fax: +972 3 641 96 83

Italy
Ente Nationale Italiano di Unificazione
Via Battistotti Sassi 11
1-20133 MILANO
Tel: +39 2 70 02 41
Fax: +39 2 70 10 61 06

Japan
Japanese Industrial Standards
Committee
c/o Standards Department Agency of
Industrial Science and Technology
Ministry of International Trade and
Industry
1-3-1, Kasumigaseki,
Chiyoda-ku
TOKYO 100
Tel: +81 3 35 01 92 95/6
Fax: +81 3 35 80 14 18

**Korea, Democratic People's
Republic of**
Committee for Standardization of the
Democratic People's Republic of Korea
Zung Gu Yok Seungli-Street
PYONGYANG
Tel: +85 02 57 15 76

Korea, Republic of
Bureau of Standards Industrial
Advancement Administration
2, Chungang-dong,
Kwachon-City
KYONGGI-DO 427-010
Tel: +82 2 503 79 38
Fax: +82 2 503 79 41

Malaysia
Standards and Industrial Research
Institute of Malaysia
Persiaran Dato' Menteri, Section 2
P.O. Box 7035, 409111 Shah Alam
SELANGOR DARUL EHSAN
Tel: +603 559 26 01
Fax: +60 3 550 80 95

Mexico
Dirección General de Normas
Calle Puente de Tecamachalco N. 6
Lomas de Tecamachaico
Sección Fuentes
Naucalpan de Juárez
53 950 MEXICO
Tel: +52 5 520 84 94
Fax: +52 5 540 51 53

Netherlands
Nederlands Normalisatie-Instituut
Kalfjeslaan 2
P.O. Box 5059
2600 GB DELFT
Tel: +31 15 69 03 90
Fax: +31 15 69 01 90

New Zealand
Standards New Zealand
Private Bag
WELLINGTON
Tel: +64 4 384 21 08
Fax: +64 4 384 39 38

Norway
Norges Standardiseringsforbund
Postboks 7020 Homansbyen
N-0306 OSLO 3
Tel: +47 22 46 60 94
Fax: +47 22 46 44 57

Pakistan
Pakistan Standards Institution
39 Garden Road, Saddar
KARACHI-74400
Tel: +92 21 722 95 27
Fax: +92 21 772 81 24

Philippines
Bureau of Product Standards
Department of Trade and Industry
361 Sen. Gil J. Puyat Avenue
Makati
METRO MANILA 1200
Tel: +63 2 817 55 27
Fax: +63 2 817 98 70

Poland
Polish Committee for Standardization,
Measures and Quality Control
Ul. Elektoraina 2
00-139 WARSZAWA
Tel: + 48 22 20 54 34
Fax: +48 22 20 83 78

Portugal
Instituto Português da Qualidade
Rua José Estavao, 83-a
P-1199 LISBOA CODEX
Tel: +351 1 52 39 78
Fax: +351 1 53 00 33

Romania
Institutul Roman de Standardizare
Str, Jean-Louis Calderon Nr. 13
Cod 70201
BUCURESTI 2
Tel: +401 611 40 43
Fax: +401 312 08 23

Russian Federation
Committee of the Russian Federation
for Standardization, Metrology and
Certification
Leninsky Prospekt 9
MOSKVA 117049
Tel: +7 095 236 40 44
Fax: +7 095 237 60 32

Saudi Arabia
Saudi Arabian Standards Organization
P.O. Box 3437
RIYADH – 11471
Tel: +966 1 479 30 46
Fax: +966 1 479 30 63

Singapore
Singapore Institute of Standards and
Industrial Research
1 Science Park Drive
SINGAPORE 0511
Tel: +65 778 77 77
Fax: +65 778 00 86

Slovakia
Slovak Office of Standards, Metrology
and Testing
Stefanovicova 3
81439 BRATISLAVA
Tel: +42 7 49 10 85
Fax: +42 7 49 10 50

South Africa
South African Bureau of Standards
Private Bag X191
PRETORIA 0001
Tel: +27 12 428 79 11
Fax: +27 12 344 15 68

Spain
Asociación Espanola de Normalización
y Certificación
Calle Fernández de la Hoz, 52
E-28010 MADRID
Tel: +34 1 310 48 51
Fax: +34 1 310 49 76

Sri Lanka
Sri Lanka Standards Institution
53 Dharmapala Mawatha
P.O. Box 17
COLOMBO 3
Tel: +94 1 22 60 51
Fax: +94 1 44 60 18

Sweden
SIS – Standardiserings-kommissionen
i Sverige
Box 3295
S-103 66 STOCKHOLM
Tel: +46 8 613 52 00
Fax: +46 8 11 70 35

Switzerland
Swiss Association for Standardization
Mühlebachstrasse 54
CH-8008 ZURICH
Tel: +41 1 254 54 54
Fax: +41 1 254 54 74

Thailand
Thai Industrial Standards Institute
Ministry of Industry
Rama VI Street
BANGKOK 10400
Tel: +66 2 245 78 02
Fax: +66 2 247 87 41

Turkey
Türk Standardlari Enstitüsü
Necatibey Cad. 112
Bakanliklar
06100 ANKARA
Tel: +90 4 417 83 30
Fax: +90 4 425 43 99

Ukraine
Ukrainian Committee for
Standardization, Metrology and
Certification
Lipskaj Street 10
252021 KIEV-21
Tel: +7 044 226 29 71
Fax: +7 044 226 29 70

United Kingdom
British Standards Institution
2 Park Street
LONDON W1A 2BS
Tel: +44 71 629 90 00
Fax: +44 71 629 05 06

USA
American National Standards Institute
11 West 42nd Street, 13th floor
NEW YORK, N.Y. 10036
Tel: +1 212 642 49 00
Fax: + 1 212 398 00 23

Venzuela
Comisión Venezolana de Normas
Industriales
Avda. Andrés Bello–
Edf. Torre Fondo Común
Piso 12
CARACAS 1050
Tel: +58 2 575 22 98
Fax: +58 2 574 13 12

Vietnam
General Departmental for
Standardization, Metrology and Quality
70, Tran Hung Dao Street
HANOI
Tel: +84 4 25 63 75
Fax: +84 4 26 52 09

Yugoslavia
Savezni zavod za standardizaciju
Kneza Milosa 20
Post. Pregr. 933
YU-11000 BEOGRAD
Tel: +38 11 68 89 99
Fax: +38 11 235 10 36

You can find a complete list of standards bodies at the back of the *Directory of quality system registration bodies*.
This is published by:

ISO Central Secretariat
Case Postale 56
CH-1211 Geneva 20
Switzerland
Tel: +44 22 749 01 11
Fax: +44 22 733 34 30.

If you need a *certification body*, the same directory lists certification bodies in country order. Not all these bodies are accredited, but ISO is working towards consistency in its listings. If you don't find a certification body listed for your country, it does not mean that none exist. Certification bodies operate across national boundaries.

Terms also vary from one country to another. In some countries, 'certification' is called 'accreditation'. ISO prefers the term 'Assessment and registration'.

Other sources of information include: your government department responsible for trade and industry, your trade association, management consultancies, libraries and business magazines.

Action List

- List the organisations you need to contact.
- When seeking information, ask:
  - What information is free (such as leaflets and guides)?
  - What information would you have to pay for (such as books or videos)?

- What services does the organisation provide (for example seminars or consultancy, and at what cost)?
- What level of expertise does the organisation have? What qualifications do its tutors or consultants have?
- What experience does the organisation have in meeting your particular needs (for example, small business or construction)?
- How long will it take to get the information or receive the service (for example what is the date of the next training course)?

■ Assess how useful the organisation will be. Ask yourself:
- What is the level of professionalism and knowledge demonstrated by the organisation's publicity material?
- What impression do you get from those with whom you come in contact (such as advisors or telephonists)? Are they efficient and friendly, or slow and pompous?
- What is the role of the organisation? Does it have something it wants you to buy?

APPENDIX 4

◆

ISO 9000 (BS 5750) Checklist

Use this checklist to see how close you are to getting ISO 9000. When you can answer 'yes' to all the questions, you will be ready for certification.

Below are the questions that the assessor will want answered. When you answer 'yes' to a question, he will promptly say, 'Show me. Prove it'. You will need to show him the relevant piece of paper. He may then enquire further, by talking to the person who actually does the job.

When you do your pre-assessment, don't accept a bland 'yes' from a department. Probe to find whether the system is really working properly.

	Yes/No	Comments
Do you have a written policy statement?		
Is the policy statement understood by all staff?		
Have you defined the responsibilities of people whose work affects quality (eg through an organisation chart or job responsibilities?		
Have you decided what checks need to be made? Are people appointed to do these checks?		
Do you do checks on inspection, production, installation, and servicing?		
Are the checks done by people who are independent of the work being checked?		
Have you appointed someone to be responsible for quality?		

	Yes/No	Comments
Is there a regular management meeting to discuss the quality system? Do you keep records of these meetings?		
Do you check orders or contracts to see that the customer's requirements are clearly defined? Do you check that you can fulfil the orders? Do you keep a record of these checks?		
Have you specified in writing who is responsible for each design and development activity? (ISO 9001 only).		
Have you planned how design work will be carried out? Have you assigned to it people who are qualified to do this work? (ISO 9001 only).		
Have you identified how other departments will work with design (such as marketing)? Have you written this down? Do you regularly review it? (ISO 9001 only).		
Have you defined in writing what needs to be in a design brief? Does the design department resolve an incomplete or conflicting brief with the person that issued it? (ISO 9001 only).		
Does the design department put its output in writing? Does it show how its designs meet the brief? (ISO 9001 only).		
Do competent people check that the designs meet the brief? Are their methods documented? (ISO 9001 only).		
Do you have a system for documenting and approving any design changes? (ISO 9001 only).		

	Yes/No	Comments
Do you control the circulation of documents which affect quality (such as manuals)? Are these documents checked by a qualified person before they are issued?		
Are up-to-date copies of quality documents available where people need them?		
Are obsolete documents promptly removed?		
Are changes to documents checked by the people who approved the original document?		
When you make changes to a document, do you state in writing why the change was made?		
Do you have a master list which shows all the changes that have been made?		
Do you re-issue documents when several changes have been made?		
Do you keep records of acceptable suppliers?		
Do you have a system for choosing suppliers?		
Do you have effective controls for checking your suppliers?		
Do your purchase orders describe the type of goods you are buying? Do you refer to a drawing, an international standard or some other reference?		
Do you check purchase orders before they go out?		
Have you specified how anything belonging to a customer will be protected? Do you record any losses and report them to the customer?		
Can you trace a product though all stages of production, if appropriate?		

	Yes/No	Comments
If traceability is a requirement, do all products or batches have a unique identification? Do you keep records of this?		
Do you have written instructions governing all processes which affect the quality of your product?		
Do you define how processes and equipment shall be monitored?		
Do you define the standards of workmanship required for your processes?		
If you make products whose effectiveness can't be checked once they have been made, do you ensure continuous monitoring during production? Do you define how this will be done? Do you keep records of this?		
Do you ensure that raw materials and other supplies are checked before use? Have you put in writing how these checks will be made?		
If you have to use raw materials urgently without their having been checked, do you identify them so that they can be recalled if found to be faulty?		
Do you inspect your products during the process as specified in your manual? Do you check that the products meet the right quality?		
Do you hold your products during processing until they have been inspected?		
Does your inspection method identify faulty goods?		
Do you do a final inspection when the product is complete? Do you check that all previous inspections have been carried out?		

	Yes/No	Comments
Do you hold products after processing until the final inspection has been made?		
Do you keep inspection records?		
Do you maintain and measuring equipment? Do you know its accuracy?		
Have you identified what measurements shall be taken, and how accurate they should be?		
Have you identified all measuring equipment? Have you calibrated it to a national standard?		
Do you have a calibration procedure, which identifies the equipment to be checked, the frequency of calibration, and the check method?		
Is your measurement equipment marked to show its calibration status?		
Do you keep calibration records?		
Do you check the validity of previous tests when calibration equipment is found to be faulty?		
Do you ensure that tests are performed in a suitable environment?		
Do you handle and store measurement equipment so as to maintain its accuracy?		
Do you safeguard measurement equipment against unauthorised adjustments?		
If you use jigs, templates or test software, do you check that it is capable of demonstrating the product's acceptability?		
Do you demonstrate that products have passed or failed tests, by stamps, tags or other means?		

	Yes/No	Comments
Do you keep records of who inspected and approved the products?		
Do you ensure that faulty products are prevented from being used? How are such products documented, evaluated, segregated and disposed of?		
Do you re-inspect faulty products which have been repaired or re-worked?		
Do you investigate the causes of faulty products and complaints?		
Do you take action to prevent these faults from recurring? Do you change your method of working as a result of taking corrective action?		
Do you handle, store, pack and deliver your products in such a way that they are not damaged?		
Do you have stock rooms? Do you have a method for receipt and delivery of goods to and from the stores?		
Do you keep quality records? Do you state how and where records shall be kept, and for how long?		
Do you keep records that show that your products are of the right quality?		
Do you carry out internal quality audits?		
Do you put in writing the results of the audits, and give them to the responsible personnel? Do they take corrective action?		
Do you identify training needs? Do you provide training? Do you keep training records?		

	Yes/No	Comments
If you provide servicing, do you have a procedure for ensuring that it meets the customer's requirements?		
Do you use statistics to demonstrate that your product is of the right quality?		

INDEX

Accreditation bodies 39–41, 48, 49,
    157; *see also* certification bodies
accuracy
    of inspection equipment 86-7, 91
    standards of in quality plans 105
adequacy audits 113–14
appeals, to certification bodies 133
assessments 110, 111, 157
    closing meetings 132–3
    cost of 128, 133
    methods of 129–30
    process of 128–33
    and re-assessment 136
    standard of assessors 132
    statistical techniques 123–4
audits 47, 110–18, 157
    first party *see* audits, internal
    internal 110, 111–18, 155, 158
        adequacy 113–14
        and checklists 115
        completion of 118
        compliance 114
        and corrective action 111, 113
        and non-conformance reports
            116–8
        purpose of 111
        questioning techniques 115
        selection of internal auditors
            111–12, 118
        setting up audit plans 112–13
        timing of 114
    pre-assessment visits 58–9, 114–15
    and quality review meetings 95–6
    second party *see* audits, supplier
    supplier 75, 110–11, 118
    third party *see* assessments

bar codes, and traceability 120
Blood Transfusion Service 68–9
Bright Plastic Panels 120–1

British Standards
    BS 5179 20, 7750 139, 141
    BS 6143, on costs of quality 125
    BS 5750, development of 20
    BS 5750 *see also* ISO 9000 (BS 5750)
British Standards Institution (BSI) 20,
    23, 163–4
    BSI QA body 24
bureaucracy, dangers of in ISO 9000
    (BS 5750) 36–7, 64
business magazines, as information
    source 168
business process re-engineering 10
BVQI (certification body) 131
    stockist scheme 24

calibration and testing information
    122, 134, 157, 167
    equipment 130
CARES (certification body) 126
case histories
    on adaptation of ISO 9000 (BS
        5750) to fit company 104–5
    on buyers' attitudes 37
    on corrective action 107–8
    on effects of lack of training 97
    of introduction of ISO 9000 (BS
        5750) 17, 18, 131
    on ISO 9000 (BS 5750) and
        paperwork 47
    on ISO 9000 saving contract 139–40
    on need for staff involvement 43–4
    on process of certification 57
    on product identification 120–1
    on quality failures 64
    on quality standards 27–8, 89–90
    on reasons for seeking certification
        33–4
    on record keeping 122–3
    on role of design 78–9

on small organisations 54
on upgrading to ISO 9001 56
category management 10
CE Mark (product standard
        requirement) 34
certification 9, 160
    choice of certification body 126,
        128, 135
    choosing right part of business for
        51–3
    choosing which part of standards to
        apply for 53–7
    costs 27
    of management consultancies 61
    process of 26–7, 126–35
    publicising achievement 48, 50,
        136–8
    and surveillance visits 27, 39, 111,
        136–7
    time needed to reach 35
certification bodies 19, 23, 24, 39, 131,
        158
    accreditation of 39–41, 48, 49, 159
    appeals to 133
    Association of British Certification
        Bodies (ABCB) 164
    choice of 126, 128, 135
    consultancy operations 41
    costs of 126, 128
    criteria for choice 47–8, 50
    Directory of Approved Suppliers
        137–8
    international 174
    listed 164–5
    National Accreditation Council for
        Certification Bodies 163
    value of 26–7
chambers of commerce 168
charities
    benefits of ISO 9000 (BS 5750) for
        33
    seeking registration 69
checklists
    by service companies 84–5
    for contract review 82
    and internal audits 115
    for preparing for ISO 9000 (BS
        5750) 176–82

    for process control 84–5
communication
    of achievement of ISO 9000 (BS
        5750) 48, 50, 136–8
    and co-operation 16
    of internal audits 117–18
    and training 96–100
competition, and benefits of ISO 9000
        (BS 5750) 26
complaints
    by customers 106–9
    costs of 125
    dealing with 89, 91
    and quality review meetings 96
compliance audits 114
computer software
    costs of poor quality 23
    Tickit standard 23, 24
construction companies
    adaptation of ISO 9000 (BS 5750)
        for 29
    benefits of ISO 9000 (BS 5750) for
        33
    quality standards 89–90
    standards of accuracy 59
consumers see customers
contract review 91
    for avoiding bad debts 82
    clauses relating to 74, 81–2
control of non-conforming products,
        clauses relating to 74
corrective action 106–9, 153
    for defective products 88–90, 152–4
    and future improvement 106–9
    and internal audits 111, 113
costs
    of assessment 133
    of certification 27
    of certification bodies 126, 128
    of complaints 125
    of ISO 9000 (BS 5750) 35
    of mistakes by suppliers 75
    of quality failures 32, 64, 71, 120–1,
        124–5
    saved by ISO 9000 (BS 5750) 31, 32
CSC-Index 23
customer care programmes 107, 139
customer supplied products 77–8, 80

customers
  benefits of ISO 9000 (BS 5750) for
      31–2
  and choice of part of ISO 9000 (BS
      5750) 55
  communicating achievement of ISO
      9000 (BS 5750) 137
  complaints by 89, 91, 106–9
  effect of ISO 9000 (BS 5750) on
      relationships with 27, 38
  questionnaires from 115
  requirements for ISO 9000 (BS
      5750) 33

debts, avoiding bad 82
defective products
  acceptability of 88, 153
  control of 152
  corrective action 88–90, 152–4
  costs of 124
  re-grading 89, 90, 153
  re-working 88, 153
  scrapping 89–90, 153
Denne Builders 47
design 134
  clauses relating to 56, 61, 74, 78–80,
      146–7
  control of 78
  establishing best practice 79–80
  and legal requirements 79
  relationship of design department
      with rest of company 78–9, 80
  structure of department 80
Dickson, Paul 14
Directory of Approved Suppliers 137–8
documents
  control of 63, 101–3, 109, 147–8
  controlled 158
  keeping up to date 95, 101–2, 103
  uncontrolled 102
  using common format 103

effectiveness, increased by ISO 9000
      (BS 5750) 32–3
efficiency, and choice of part of ISO
      9000 (BS 5750) 55, 56
employees see staff

EN 29000 (European quality standard)
      158
  development of 21
  see also ISO 9000 (BS 5750)
European quality standards 18, 21, 158
  CE Mark 34
  see also under ISO 9000 (BS 5750)
export marketing, and ISO 9000 (BS
      5750) 31

faults see corrective action; defective
      products; inspection;
      non-conformance
Ford Motor Company 139, 140
free issue goods 77–8, 80
Fridays (Cranbrook) Ltd 67, 68

goods inward inspection 75, 86, 150
grants, from Department of Trade and
      Industry 162
guidelines for specific industries 168–9

Halton General Hospital, Electro-Bio
      Medical Engineering Unit 28–9
handling and storage of products 90,
      91, 154
  clauses relating to 74
Harris, Val 104
health and safety regulations 79

identification of products 119–21, 125,
      134, 149
in-process inspection 86
inspection 91
inspection and testing 150–1
  clauses relating to 74
  equipment for 86–7, 91, 122, 151–2
  final 86, 151
  improvements in reducing errors
      85–90
  in-process 86
  and ISO 9003 (BS 5750 Part 3) 22
  of purchases 86
  as quality management strategy
      14–15
  and record keeping 151
  regular 63
  of 'special processes' 85

staffing requirements 29
internal audits *see* audits, internal
International Organisation for
    Standardization (ISO) 20
  Directory of quality system registration
    bodies 174
international standards addresses listed
    169–74
  Directory of quality system registration
    bodies 174
ISO 9000 (BS 5750)
  auditing systems *see* audits
  benchmarks 48–9, 50
  benefits of 9, 10, 24, 30–5, 134
  building on 138–40, 141
  certification procedure *see*
    certification
  and clarification of responsibilities
    45, 62, 144
  compliance of manuals 113–14, 128,
    135
  components of 17
  on controlling production process
    149–50
  and corrective action *see* corrective
    action
  costs of 35
  criticism of 19, 25–8
  and customer relationships 27, 38
  customer requirements for 33
  dangers of bureaucracy 29, 36–7, 38,
    64
  definition of quality 14
  describing company processes 45–6
  on design 146–7
  disadvantages 35–7, 38
  on document control 101, 147–8
  effectiveness increased by 32–3
  effects of 35
  failures in 36
  flexibility of 18
  glossary of terms 157–61
  on handling and storage of products
    154
  history 20
  implementation of 41–8
    advantages of company installing
      57

  creating plans 48
  setting of quality levels 30
  setting up committee 49
  setting up ISO 9000 group 43
  use of ready-made manuals 57–8,
    61
  on inspection equipment 86–7, 151–2
  on inspection and testing *see*
    inspection and testing
  on internal audits *see* audits
  international use of 21
  lack of definitive version 19
  language of 62, 99, 143, 157–61
  logo 138, 141
  and low standards 25, 27–8, 38
  on management responsibility 95,
    143
  meaning of 9
  on order checking 145
  on organisation 144
  paperwork generated by 29, 47
  Part 1 (ISO 9001) 22, 53–7, 74, 80
  Part 2 (ISO 9002) 22, 53–7, 74, 91
  Part 3 (ISO 9003) 22
  Parts 1 and 2 compared 143
  preparation checklist 176–82
  on preventative action 153–4
  principles of
    carrying out regular checks 63
    communication 63
    controlling key documents 63
    identifying and correcting faults
      63, 71
    keeping records *see* record keeping
    organisation 62
    writing procedures *see* procedures
  problems of 9, 19, 24
  on product identification *see* product
    identification
  and production of approved
    suppliers list 75
  on purchasing 148–9
  and quality plans 106
  on quality records 155
  on quality system 144–5
  reasons for failure to achieve 134–5
  reasons for seeking 133, 135
  on record keeping *see* record keeping

registration requirements *see*
  certification
resistance to 26, 36, 44, 98
on servicing 91, 156
and software companies 23
staff commitment to *see* staff
staff requirements 29, 35, 38
on statistical techniques 156
stockist scheme 23-4
structure of 72-4, 143-56
  information clauses 72, 73
  staff clauses 72, 73
  systems clauses 72, 73
  work clauses 72-80
time need for implementation 35-6,
  48
on training 96-100, 155-6

Jackson and Ashton, *Implementing
  Quality through BS 5750* 168
Jaguar Cars 139
  increase in reliability ratings 79-80
Japan
  relationship between purchasers and
    suppliers 75
  trade with 131
job cards, and product identification
  119
job descriptions 92-3
  advantages of 93
  disadvantages of 93

low standards
  costs of 64
  and ISO 9000 (BS 5750) 25, 27-8,
    38
low standards *see also* defective
  products; non conformance
LVS Rubber Mouldings 131

management
  checks on quality system 95-6
  commitment to ISO 9000 (BS 5750)
    135, 140
  responsibilities of 143, 144
management consultancies 39, 49, 57,
  167
  action list for checking 60-1

advantages of using 58-9, 61
assessment of 59-61
certification of 61
costs of 27
pre-assessment visits by 58-9, 114
problems with 59, 61
and staff involvement 59, 60
use of ready-made manuals 58
management reviews 159
manuals 160
  auditing adequacy of 113-14
  avoiding unnecessary length 69-70
  compliance with ISO 9000 (BS
    5750) 128, 135
  computer-based 64-5
  and document control 102-3
  exclusion of unnecessary clauses
    103-5, 109
  levels of 65-6, 71
  policy *see* manuals, system
  procedures 66-8
  ready-made 57-8, 61
  setting up 64-70
  system 66
  work instructions 68
manufacturing companies
  effect of lack of systems on 11-13
  quality checks 14
market developments, and quality
  review meetings 96
measurement, national standards of 87,
  91
military standards
  benefits of 81-2
  and development of ISO 9000 (BS
    5750) 20, 24, 81
mistakes, preventing repetition 16
motor industry, use of ISO 9000 (BS
  5750) 139-40
Murphy Group (construction
  company) 104-5

National Accreditation Council for
  Certification Bodies (NACCB)
  39-40, 163
National Measurement Accreditation
  Service (NAMAS) 87, 167
National Physical Laboratory, and

national standards of
measurement 87
National Registration Scheme for
Assessors of Quality Systems
112
newsletters, coverage of ISO 9000 (BS
5750) in 99, 100, 137
non-conformance 89, 90, 129, 159
major 130–1, 132
of manuals 128
minor 130, 131, 132
reports 116–18
and system failures 131
use of audits to resolve 96
Norgren Martonair, benefits of
introducing ISO 9000 (BS
5750) 17
Northern Electric 107–8
nursing homes, process control 84

Oasters (egg producers), certification
process 57
order checking 145
order processing 81–2
organisation charts 92, 93, 94
Outset (computer training charity)
69–70

paperwork, generated by ISO 9000
(BS 5750) 29, 36–7, 64
partnership sourcing 10, 75
PECS (certification body) 126
personnel see staff
Peters, Tom 17
The Pursuit of Excellence 37
photocopying of uncontrolled
documents 102
pre-assessment audits 58–9, 114–15
press releases, on achieving ISO 9000
(BS 5750) 137
preventative action 153–4
Price Waterhouse 23
procedures
need for simplicity and clarity 70–1
updating 103
writing of 44, 46, 62–3, 70–1
see also documents
procedures manuals 66–8

process control 83–5, 91, 150
clauses relating to 74
statistical 139
Procter and Gamble, customer care
lines 106
product identification 119–21, 125,
134, 149
product liability claims, and ISO 9000
(BS 5750) 31
production process, control of 149–50
projects, quality plans for 105–6, 109
public sector, traceability in 120
publicity 140–1
on achieving ISO 9000 (BS 5750)
48, 50, 136–8
purchase orders, completion of 76, 80
purchasers 159; see also customers
purchasing
changing the order 77–8
clauses relating to 74–8
goods inward inspection 75

quality
definition of 14
methods of checking 14–15
responsibility for and ISO 9000 (BS
5750) 16
Quality Assurance, Institute of 97
quality assurance (QA) 15, 24, 159
resolution of quality problems 16
see also ISO 9000 (BS 5750)
quality bodies
Association of Quality Management
Consultants (AQMC) 166–7
Institute of Quality Assurance (IQA)
166
National Quality Information Centre
(NQIC) 166
Quality Methods Association
(QMA) 166
quality control (QC) 14–15, 24, 159
in ISO 9000 (BS 5750) 16
quality failures 12–13
costs of 32, 64, 71, 120–1, 124–5
quality management
failure 14–15
inspection 14–15
prevention 14, 15

quality managers 135, 159
    choice of 94, 100
    costs of 124
    production of audit reports 118
    role of 41–3, 49, 94–5
    training of 112
quality manuals *see* manuals
quality plans, for projects 105–6, 109,
    160
quality policies 160
    writing of 44–5
quality problems, resolution of by
        quality assurance 16
quality records 155
quality review meetings 95–6, 100
questioning techniques, in internal
        audits 115
questionnaires
    from certification bodies 126
    from customers 115

Radiographers, Institute of 125
receiving inspection 86
record keeping 63, 121–3, 145
    assessment of 121–2
    on computer 122, 155
    and document control 147–8
    on inspection 151
    of inspection equipment 87
    for internal audits 112–13
    as legal protection 85
    necessity of 44
    and product identification 121
    purchase orders 76, 80
    in quality plans 105
    and responsibilities of quality
            manager 94–5
    and surveillance visits 136
    of use of ISO 9000 (BS 5750) 17
registration *see* certification
remedial action *see* corrective action
report writing, standardisation of 29
responsibilities, clarification of by ISO
        9000 (BS 5750) 45, 62, 144
roles, defining 92–4
Rolls Royce 140

St Joseph and St Teresa School,
        corrective action 108
serial numbers, and product
        identification 119
service companies
    adaptation of ISO 9000 (BS 5750)
        for 29–30
    assessment of suppliers 76
    checking procedures for key stages
        88
    choosing departments for
        certification 52
    dealing with customer complaints
        89, 91, 106–9
    effect of lack of systems on 12–13
    process control 84
    quality checks 14–15
    servicing by 91
    traceability 119–20
    use of checklists 84–5
servicing 156
    clause relating to 74, 91
    documentation of 91
SGS Yarsley, survey of cost benefits
        of ISO 9000 (BS 5750) 32
Siemens Lighting, introduction of ISO
        9001 (BS 5750 Part I) 56
slogans, ineffectiveness of 99
small businesses
    adoption of ISO 9000 (BS 5750)
        28–9
    costs of certification 27
Smith, Roger, on preparing for
        assessment 131–2
Solicitors' Indemnity Fund 125
'special processes' 91
    checking of 85
specifications, and ISO 9000 (BS
        5750) 16
staff
    benefits of ISO 9000 (BS 5750) for
        30–1
    and compliance audits 114
    defining roles 92–4
    involvement of 44, 96–100
        and management consultancies 59,
            60
        in quality system 133

in writing procedures 46, 49, 70–1
out-workers and home-workers 98
requirements of ISO 9000 (BS 5750)
    relating to 35, 38, 41–3, 72
training of 96–100, 155–6
statistical process control 139
statistical techniques 123–5, 156
stockists, ISO 9000 (BS 5750) scheme
    for 23–4
storage and handling of products 90,
    91,134, 154
sub-contractors 160
suppliers
    acceptability of 28
    assessing quality of 74
    corrective action by 75
    Directory of Approved Suppliers
        137–8
    improving quality of 74–7
    production of approved suppliers
        list 75
    for service companies 76
    strengths and weaknesses of 28
surveillance bodies 140
surveillance visits 27, 39, 111, 136–7
    cost of 128
system manuals 66; *see also* manuals

systems, effect of lack of 11–13

Taylor, John 17
Tickit standard for computer software
    23, 24
TQM (Total Quality Management)
    139, 141
traceability 125, 160
    in public sector 120
    in service companies 119–20
Trada (certification body) 126
trade associations 167–8
Trade and Industry, Department of
    (DTI) 23, 162–3
    QA Register 168
training 16, 96–100, 155–6
    explaining system to staff 97–8
    failures in 97
    of internal auditors 112
Training and Enterprise Companies
    (TECs) 163

uncontrolled documents 102

work instructions 161
    manuals 68